SLAUGHTERHOUSE

SLAUGHTERHOUSE

Maris Kreizman

FLATIRON
BOOKS
NEW YORK

SLAUGHTERHOUSE 90210. Copyright © 2015 by Maris Kreizman. All rights reserved.
Printed in China. For information, address Flatiron Books, 175 Fifth Avenue,
New York, N.Y. 10010.

www.flatironbooks.com

The credits and permissions that appear on pages 209–213 constitute a
continuation of the copyright page.

Designed by Elizabeth Van Itallie

The Library of Congress Cataloging-in-Publication Data is available upon request.

ISBN 978-1-250-06110-2 (hardcover)
ISBN 978-1-250-06112-6 (e-book)

Flatiron books may be purchased for educational, business, or promotional use.
For information on bulk purchases, please contact the Macmillan Corporate
and Premium Sales Department at 1-800-221-7945, extension 5442, or write to
specialmarkets@macmillan.com.

First Edition: October 2015

10 9 8 7 6 5 4 3 2 1

To Mom and Dad with love and gratitude

INTRODUCTION

I read for pleasure and that is the moment I learn the most.
—Margaret Atwood

It all started with a poignant scene from the semiscripted show *The Hills*, as many great intellectual undertakings do. The heroine and moral center of the not-quite-reality show that ran on MTV from 2006 to 2010 and preceded the rise of *Real Housewives*–esque wealth-porn TV was Lauren Conrad, a mega-privileged California girl with tons of wonderful opportunities, a beautiful apartment, great hair, and really bad taste in boys and friends. The entire show had a fake, airbrushed glow about it, but Lauren's emotions always seemed so real. She *felt* things. There's a famous screenshot from *The Hills* that shows Conrad arguing with a friend over some petty yet dramatic grievance and crying the most perfect single black mascara tear.

As I watched that gorgeous tear fall in slow motion, I thought of a quote from a novel I'd recently read: "Never did anybody look so sad. Bitter and black, halfway down, in the darkness, in the shaft which ran from the sunlight to the depths, perhaps a tear formed; a tear fell; the waves swayed this way and that, received it, and were at rest. Never did anybody look so sad." It's an observation from Virginia Woolf's *To the Lighthouse* made by the matriarch of a large family about a young homesick maid in her service. It's a passing thought, a tiny vivid portrait in the midst of a much larger stream-of-consciousness narrative that flicks between topics like the remote control of an avid channel surfer. The impression of LC's (as she's known to her fans) angst struck me in a similar way. *Click.*

We all know the thrill of reading a great line that illuminates an idea we've sensed but were unable to articulate, that magical feeling when a piece of writing leads us to see the world with greater clarity or more wonder. Such epiphanies can be inspired by TV shows and pop songs and films as much as books, of course. Pop culture and literature are not mutually exclusive passions. In fact, they work in tandem. Media from every area of the spectrum can edify and influence us, and there are a zillion shades of gray within culture—there is so much fluidity between high and low. So of course Daria Morgendorffer, Whitney Houston, and Alex P. Keaton can inform our ways of thinking just as much as Sylvia Plath or James Baldwin ever could. The Fly Girls from *In Living Color* could be childhood inspirations just as much as Louisa May Alcott's March girls. Our brains can be equal parts George Eliot and George Costanza, Jean-Paul Sartre and Mark-Paul Gosselaar, both Jane Austen's Emma and *Clueless*'s Cher Horowitz.

What a delight to discover, then, that one of the greatest living writers of our time, Lorrie Moore, could inadvertently explain the appeal of *America's Funniest Home Videos* and *Jackass*: "I have always felt that life is a series of personal humiliations relieved, occasionally, by the humiliations of others." Or that the antiheroes who populate so many of TV's most prestigious dramas—Omar Little, Tony Soprano, Walter White—echo the sentiments of the narrator of P. G. Wodehouse's 1906 novel, *Love Among the Chickens*: "I am not always good and noble. I am the hero of this story, but I have my off moments."

Looking through the lens of literature, you might discover that Hemingway expresses heartache in *The Sun Also Rises* just as palpably as *My So-Called Life* does, or that you might like Daphne du Maurier if you are completely obsessed with the Hitchcockian nighttime soap *Pretty Little Liars*. You might find that Veronica Mars or Lisa Simpson are feminist icons just as much as Susan Sontag is, or that *Orange Is the New Black* is a natural successor to Russian epics by Tolstoy and Dostoyevsky, or that Leslie Knope of *Parks and Recreation* could have been a Jane Austen heroine.

Since 2009, *Slaughterhouse 90210* has been celebrating the intersection of literature and pop culture. What started as a goofy mash-up designed to compare and contrast high and low culture to comedic effect (in retrospect, pairing F. Scott Fitzgerald with *Jersey Shore* in 2009 seems portentous of Snooki's 2014 *Gatsby*-themed wedding) evolved into a larger, more diverse project that aims to inspire lovers of culture to binge read as much as they binge watch shows and films on Netflix. Great writing transcends time and place and is even more essential in our Internet-addled, DVR-addicted age than it ever was.

EVERYTHING WAS BEAUTIFUL AND NOTHING HURT.
—Kurt Vonnegut, *Slaughterhouse-Five*

It is curious what patches of hardness and tenderness lie side by side in men's dispositions. I suppose he has some test by which he finds out whom Heaven cares for.

—George Eliot, *Middlemarch*

Coherence and closure are deep human desires that are presently unfashionable. But they are always both frightening and enchantingly desirable. "Falling in love," characteristically, combs the appearances of the word, and of the particular lover's history, out of a random tangle and into a coherent plot.

—A. S. Byatt, *Possession*

Life is an endless recruiting of witnesses. It seems we need to be observed in our postures of extravagance or shame, we need attention paid to us. Our own memory is altogether too cherishing, which is the kindest thing I can say for it. Other accounts are required, other perspectives, but even so our most important ceremonies—birth, love, and death—are secured by whomever and whatever is available. What chance, what caprice!

—Carol Shields, *The Stone Diaries*

Above all, she is the girl who "feels" things, who has hung on to the freshness and pain of adolescence, the girl ever wounded, ever young.

—Joan Didion, *Slouching Towards Bethlehem*

A man's subconscious self
is not the ideal companion.
It lurks for the greater part
of his life in some dark den
of its own, hidden away,
and emerges only to taunt
and deride and increase the
misery of a miserable hour.

—P. G. Wodehouse, *The Adventures of Sally*

When you find out who you are, you will no longer be innocent. That will be sad for others to see. All that knowledge will show on your face and change it. But sad only for others, not for yourself. You will feel you have a kind of wisdom, very mistaken, but a mistake of some power to you and so you will sadly treasure it and grow it.

—Lorrie Moore, *A Gate at the Stairs*

Yet, I didn't understand that she was intentionally disguising her feelings with sarcasm; that was usually the last resort of people who are timid and chaste of heart, whose souls have been coarsely and impudently invaded; and who, until the last moment, refuse to yield out of pride and are afraid to express their own feelings to you.

—Fyodor Dostoyevsky, *Notes from Underground*

I HAVE AN IDEA THAT THE ONLY THING WHICH MAKES IT POSSIBLE TO REGARD THIS WORLD WE LIVE IN WITHOUT DISGUST IS THE BEAUTY WHICH NOW AND THEN MEN CREATE OUT OF THE CHAOS.

—W. Somerset Maugham, *The Painted Veil*

I GUESS THIS IS WHAT MARRIAGE IS, OR WAS, OR COULD BE. YOU DROP THE MASK. YOU ALLOW THE FATIGUE IN. YOU LEAN ACROSS AND KISS THE YEARS BECAUSE THEY'RE THE THINGS THAT MATTER.

—Colum McCann, *Let the Great World Spin*

A rowdy bunch on the whole, they were most of them so violently individualistic as to be practically interchangeable.

—Elaine Dundy, *The Dud Avocado*

It doesn't matter what you do. In the end, you are going to be judged, and all the times that you're not at your most dignified are the ones that will be recalled in all their vivid, heartbreaking detail. And then of course these things will be distorted and exaggerated and replayed over and over, until eventually they turn into the essence of you: your cartoon.

—Dan Chaon, *Among the Missing*

AT THE AGE OF ELEVEN OR THEREABOUTS
WOMEN ACQUIRE A POISE AND AN ABILITY
TO HANDLE DIFFICULT SITUATIONS WHICH A
MAN, IF HE IS LUCKY, MANAGES TO ACHIEVE
SOMEWHERE IN THE LATER SEVENTIES.

—P. G. Wodehouse, *Uneasy Money*

For most of us, the experience of love, even if it doesn't work out—perhaps especially when it doesn't work out—promises that here is one thing that validates, that vindicates life. And though subsequent years might alter this view, until some of us give up on it altogether, when love first strikes there's nothing like it, is there? Agreed?

—Julian Barnes, *The Sense of an Ending*

People want to be bowled over by something special. Nine times out of ten you can forget, but that tenth time, that peak experience, is what people want. That's what can move the world. That's art.

—Haruki Murakami, *South of the Border, West of the Sun*

There are levels of readiness. Young girls don't entertain the idea of sex, their body and another's together. That comes later, but there isn't nothing before. There's an innocent displacement, a dreaming, and idols are perfect for a little girl's dreaming.

—Rachel Kushner, *The Flamethrowers*

Privilege, you see, is one of the great adversaries of the imagination; it spreads a thick layer of adipose tissue over our sensitivity.

—Chinua Achebe, *Hopes and Impediments: Selected Essays*

I MEET A PERSON, AND IN MY MIND I'M SAYING THREE MINUTES; I GIVE YOU THREE MINUTES TO SHOW ME THE SPARK.

—*The Collected Stories of Amy Hempel*

As he took her hand she saw him look her over from head
to foot, a gesture she recognized and that made her feel
at home, but gave her always a faint feeling of superiority
to whoever made it. If her person was property she could
exercise whatever advantage was inherent in its ownership.

—F. Scott Fitzgerald, *Tender Is the Night*

VAIN TRIFLES AS THEY SEEM, CLOTHES HAVE, THEY SAY, MORE IMPORTANT OFFICES THAN TO MERELY KEEP US WARM. THEY CHANGE OUR VIEW OF THE WORLD AND THE WORLD'S VIEW OF US.

—Virginia Woolf, *Orlando*

What is interesting and important happens mostly in secret, in places where there is no power. Nothing much of lasting value ever happens at the head table, held together by a familiar rhetoric. Those who already have power continue to glide along the familiar rut they have made for themselves.

—Michael Ondaatje, *The Cat's Table*

Many kids, it seemed, would find out that their parents were flawed, messed-up people later in life, and I didn't appreciate getting to know it all so strong and early.

—Aimee Bender, *The Particular Sadness of Lemon Cake*

LA GRANGE PARK PUBLIC
LIBRARY DISTRICT

MATT GROENING

She was always planning out her own development, desiring her own perfection, observing her own progress. Her nature had for her own imagination a certain garden-like quality, a suggestion of perfume and murmuring bows, of shady bowers and of lengthening vistas, which made her feel that introspection was, after all, an exercise in the open air, and that a visit to the recesses of one's mind was harmless when one returned from it with a lapful of roses.

—Henry James, *The Portrait of a Lady*

Love demands expression. It will not stay still, stay silent, be good, be modest, be seen and not heard, no. It will break out in tongues of praise, the high note that smashes the glass and spills the liquid.

—Jeanette Winterson, *Written on the Body*

IT OFTEN HAPPENS THAT THINGS ARE OTHER THAN WHAT THEY SEEM, AND YOU CAN GET YOURSELF INTO TROUBLE BY JUMPING TO CONCLUSIONS.

—Paul Auster, *Moon Palace*

She discovered with great delight that one does not love one's children just because they are one's children but because of the friendship formed while raising them.

—Gabriel García Márquez, *Love in the Time of Cholera*

Whenever I saw her, I felt like I had been living in another country, doing moderately well in another language, and then she showed up speaking English and suddenly I could speak with all the complexity and nuance that I hadn't realized was gone. With Lucy I was a native speaker.

—Ann Patchett, *Truth & Beauty*

She had the air of a supervisor, a cheerful but vigilant overseer—or perhaps the air of a woman who would assume that role whether she had any official superiority or not.

Let truth be told—women do as a rule live through such humiliations, and regain their spirits, and again look about them with an interested eye. While there's life there's hope is a conviction not so entirely unknown to the "betrayed" as some amiable theorists would have us believe.

—Thomas Hardy, *Tess of the d'Urbervilles*

Happiness was different in childhood. It was so much then a matter simply of accumulation, of taking things—new experiences, new emotions—and applying them like so many polished tiles to what would someday be the marvellously finished pavilion of the self.

—John Banville, *The Sea*

HUMAN MADNESS IS OFTENTIMES A CUNNING AND MOST FELINE THING. WHEN YOU THINK IT FLED, IT MAY HAVE BUT BECOME TRANSFIGURED INTO SOME STILL SUBTLER FORM.
—Herman Melville, *Moby-Dick*

There is so much hurt in this game of searching for a
mate, of testing, trying. And you realize suddenly
that you forgot it was a game, and turn away in tears.

—*The Unabridged Journals of Sylvia Plath*

In the little world in which children have their existence, whosoever brings them up, there is nothing so finely perceived and so finely felt as injustice.

—Charles Dickens, *Great Expectations*

Although I have
never been an actor
in the strict sense
of the word, I have
nevertheless in real
life always carried
about with me a small
folding theatre and
have appeared in
more than one part.

—Vladimir Nabokov,
Despair

Imagination, of course, can open any door—
turn the key and let terror walk right in.

—Truman Capote, *In Cold Blood*

An infinity of passion can be contained in
one minute, like a crowd in a small space.

—Gustave Flaubert, *Madame Bovary*

WITHIN THE SOULS OF THE AWKWARD AND THE OVERLOOKED OFTEN BURNS SOMETHING RADIANT.

—Jo Ann Beard, *In Zanesville*

Look at me. My concerns—
are they spiritual, do you
think, or carnal? Come on.
We've read our Shakespeare.

—*The Collected Stories of
Amy Hempel*

There are no conditions to which a person cannot grow accustomed,
especially if he sees that everyone around him lives in the same way.

—Leo Tolstoy, *Anna Karenina*

We are such inward secret creatures, that inwardness is the most amazing thing about us, even more amazing than our reason. But we cannot just walk into the cavern and look around. Most of what we think we know about our minds is pseudo-knowledge. We are all such shocking poseurs, so good at inflating the importance of what we think we value.

—Iris Murdoch, *The Sea, the Sea*

"I FEEL LIKE PEOPLE ACCEPT THE FIRST THING I SHOW THEM," SHE SAID, "AND THAT'S ALL I EVER AM TO THEM."
—Mary Gaitskill, *Don't Cry*

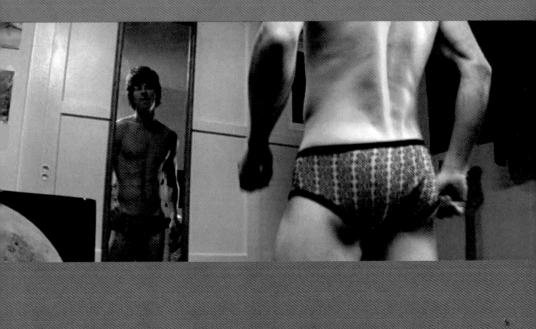

**EVERY HERO BECOMES
A BORE AT LAST.**
—Ralph Waldo Emerson,
*Representative Men: Seven
Lectures*

Who has not asked himself at some time or other: am I a monster or is this what it means to be a person?

—Clarice Lispector, *The Hour of the Star*

Anyone too undisciplined, too self-righteous or too self-centered to live in the world as it is has a tendency to idealize a world which ought to be. But no matter what political or religious direction such idealists choose, their visions always share one telling characteristic: in their utopias, heavens or brave new worlds, their greatest personal weakness suddenly appears to be a strength.

—David James Duncan,
The Brothers K

I UNDERSTOOD THAT IN THIS SMALL SPACE OF TIME WE HAD MUTUALLY SURRENDERED OUR LONELINESS AND REPLACED IT WITH TRUST.

—Patti Smith, *Just Kids*

And what made these heart-to-hearts possible—you might even say what made the whole friendship possible during that time—was this understanding we had that anything we told each other during these moments would be treated with careful respect.

—Kazuo Ishiguro, *Never Let Me Go*

All male friendships are essentially quixotic: they last only
so long as each man is willing to polish the shaving-bowl
helmet, climb on his donkey, and ride off after the other in
pursuit of illusive glory and questionable adventure.

—Michael Chabon, *Wonder Boys*

The challenge is to resist circumstances. Any idiot can be happy in a happy place, but moral courage is required to be happy in a hellhole.

—Joyce Carol Oates, *Mudwoman*

AS A GENERAL RULE, PEOPLE, EVEN THE WICKED,
ARE MUCH MORE NAIVE AND SIMPLE-HEARTED THAN
WE SUPPOSED. AND WE OURSELVES ARE, TOO.
—Fyodor Dostoyevsky, *The Brothers Karamazov*

All things truly wicked start from innocence.

—Ernest Hemingway, *A Moveable Feast*

Humor is what happens when we're told the truth quicker and more directly than we're used to.

—George Saunders, *The Braindead Megaphone*

**HOW OLD DO
YOU HAVE TO GET
BEFORE WISDOM
DESCENDS LIKE
A PLASTIC BAG
OVER YOUR HEAD
AND YOU LEARN
TO KEEP YOUR
BIG MOUTH SHUT?
MAYBE NEVER.
MAYBE YOU GET
MORE FRIVOLOUS
WITH AGE.**

—Margaret Atwood,
The Robber Bride

Some of our loves and attachments are elemental and beyond our choosing, and for that very reason they come spiced with pain and regret and need and hollowness and a feeling as close to anger as I will ever be able to imagine.

—Colm Tóibín, *Mothers and Sons*

But after a moment the sense of waste and ruin overcame him. There they were, close together and safe and shut in; yet so chained to their separate destinies that they might as well have been half the world apart.

—Edith Wharton, *The Age of Innocence*

This is what I thought: for the most banal event to become an adventure, you must (and this is enough) begin to recount it.

—Jean-Paul Sartre, *Nausea*

I believe that one can never leave home. I believe that one carries the shadows, the dreams, the fears and the dragons of home under one's skin, at the extreme corners of one's eyes and possibly in the gristle of the earlobe.

—Maya Angelou, *Letter to My Daughter*

I was tired of so much thinking, which is what I did most in those days. I did other things, but I went on thinking while I did them. I might feel something, but I would think about what I was feeling at the same time. I even had to think about what I was thinking and wonder why I was thinking about it.

—Lydia Davis, *Almost No Memory*

If you want to think about something really funny, kiddo, consider the fact that our favorite modern bad guys became villains by serving as heroes first—to millions. It is now a necessary apprenticeship.

—William H. Gass, *The Tunnel*

What if one happens to be possessed of a heart that can't be trusted—? What if the heart, for its own unfathomable reasons, leads one willfully and in a cloud of unspeakable radiance away from health, domesticity, civic responsibility and strong social connections and all the blandly-held common virtues and instead straight towards a beautiful flare of ruin, self-immolation, disaster?

—Donna Tartt, *The Goldfinch*

WHAT'S FRIENDSHIP'S REALEST MEASURE? I'LL TELL YOU. THE AMOUNT OF PRECIOUS TIME YOU'LL SQUANDER ON SOMEONE ELSE'S CALAMITIES AND FUCK-UPS.

—Richard Ford, *The Sportswriter*

It's a very Greek idea, and a very profound one. Beauty is terror. Whatever we call beautiful, we quiver before it. And what could be more terrifying and beautiful, to souls like the Greeks or our own, than to lose control completely? To throw off the chains of being for an instant, to shatter the accident of our mortal selves?

—Donna Tartt, *The Secret History*

We are so convinced of the goodness of ourselves, and the goodness of our love, we cannot bear to believe that there might be something more worthy of love than us, more worthy of worship. Greeting cards routinely tell us everybody deserves love. No. Everybody deserves clean water. Not everybody deserves love all the time.

—Zadie Smith, *White Teeth*

A most mediocre person can be the object of a love which is wild, extravagant, and beautiful as the poison lilies of the swamp.

—Carson McCullers, *The Ballad of the Sad Café*

But in life, a tragedy is not one long scream. It includes everything that led up to it. Hour after trivial hour, day after day, year after year, and then the sudden moment: the knife stab, the shell burst, the plummet of the car from a bridge.

—Margaret Atwood, *The Blind Assassin*

Now I know what a ghost is. Unfinished business, that's what.

—Salman Rushdie, *The Satanic Verses*

If trouble comes when
you least expect it then
maybe the thing to do is
to always expect it.

—Cormac McCarthy,
The Road

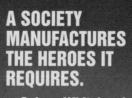

**A SOCIETY
MANUFACTURES
THE HEROES IT
REQUIRES.**

—Colson Whitehead,
Zone One

A man's power is in the half-light, in the half-seen movements of his hand and the unguessed-at expression of his face. It is the absence of facts that frightens people: the gap you open, into which they pour their fears, fantasies, desires.

—Hilary Mantel, *Wolf Hall*

THERE WERE MOMENTS WHEN HE LOOKED ON EVIL SIMPLY AS A MODE THROUGH WHICH HE COULD REALIZE HIS CONCEPTION OF THE BEAUTIFUL.

—Oscar Wilde, *The Picture of Dorian Gray*

We are dancing animals. How beautiful it is to get up and go out and do something. We are here on Earth to fart around. Don't let anybody tell you any different.

—Kurt Vonnegut, *A Man Without a Country*

It was miraculous. It was almost no trick at all, he saw, to turn vice into virtue and slander into truth, impotence into abstinence, arrogance into humility, plunder into philanthropy, thievery into honor, blasphemy into wisdom, brutality into patriotism, and sadism into justice. Anybody could do it; it required no brains at all. It merely required no character.

—Joseph Heller, *Catch-22*

YOU NEVER REALLY UNDERSTAND A PERSON
UNTIL YOU CONSIDER THINGS FROM HIS
POINT OF VIEW—UNTIL YOU CLIMB INTO HIS
SKIN AND WALK AROUND IN IT.

—Harper Lee, *To Kill a Mockingbird*

I was pulled this way and that for longer than I can remember. And my problem was that I always tried to go in everyone's way but my own. I have also been called one thing and then another while no one really wished to hear what I called myself. So after years of trying to adopt the opinions of others I finally rebelled.

—Ralph Ellison, *Invisible Man*

It contributes greatly towards a man's moral and intellectual health, to be brought into habits of companionship with individuals unlike himself, who care little for his pursuits, and whose sphere and abilities he must go out of himself to appreciate.

—Nathaniel Hawthorne, *The Scarlet Letter*

A monster. You and your friends, all of you. Pretty monsters. It's a stage all girls go through. If you're lucky you get through it without doing any permanent damage to yourself or anyone else.

—Kelly Link, *Pretty Monsters*

THE JUSTICE I HAVE RECEIVED, I SHALL GIVE BACK.
—Patricia Highsmith, *The Glass Cell*

> **Fearlessness in those without power is maddening to those who have it.**
> —Tobias Wolff, *This Boy's Life*

The truth is always an insult or a joke, lies are generally tastier. We love them. The nature of lies is to please. Truth has no concern for anyone's comfort.

—Katherine Dunn, *Geek Love*

The real marriage of true minds is for any two people to possess a sense of humor or irony pitched in exactly the same key, so that their joint glances on any subject cross like interarching searchlights.

—Edith Wharton, *A Backward Glance*

She was so much
a personality and
so little anything
else that even
staring straight
at her he had no
idea what she
really looked like.

—Jonathan
Franzen, *The
Corrections*

No, he is not tactful, yet have you ever noticed that there are people who do things which are most indelicate, and yet, at the same time, beautiful?

—E. M. Forster, *A Room with a View*

She was happy, and perfectly in line with the tradition of those women they used to call "ruined," "fallen," feckless, bitches in heat, ravished dolls, sweet sluts, instant princesses, hot numbers, great lays, succulent morsels, everybody's darlings . . .

—Jean Genet, *Querelle*

IT IS LOVE AND FRIENDSHIP, THE SANCTITY AND CELEBRATION OF OUR RELATIONSHIPS, THAT NOT ONLY SUPPORT A GOOD LIFE, BUT CREATE ONE. THROUGH FRIENDSHIPS, WE SPARK AND INSPIRE ONE ANOTHER'S AMBITIONS.

—Wallace Stegner, *Crossing to Safety*

The things we admire in men, kindness and generosity, openness, honesty, understanding and feeling, are the concomitants of failure in our system. And those traits we detest, sharpness, greed, acquisitiveness, meanness, egotism and self-interest, are the traits of success. And while men admire the quality of the first they love the produce of the second.

—John Steinbeck, *Cannery Row*

Result of self-consciousness: audience and actor are the same. I live my life as a spectacle for myself, for my own edification. I live my life but I don't live in it. The hoarding instinct in human relations.

—Susan Sontag, *Reborn: Journals and Notebooks, 1947–1963*

CAUSING ACTIVE ONGOING PLEASURE IN YOUR MATE IS SOMETHING PEOPLE TEND TO RESTRICT TO THE SEXUAL REALM OR GETTING ATTRACTIVE FOOD ON THE TABLE ON TIME, BUT KEEP- ING PERMANENT INTIMATE COMEDY GOING IS MORE IM- PORTANT THAN ANY OTHER ONE THING.

—Norman Rush, *Mating*

We were growing up. It was one of those moments when you could
practically feel the adult pushing out, pushing forward into the world.

—Hannah Pittard, *The Fates Will Find Their Way*

She recognized that this is how friendships begin: one person reveals a moment of strangeness, and the other person decides just to listen and not exploit it.

—Meg Wolitzer, *The Interestings*

If I had to sum up what he did to me, I'd say it was this: he made me sing along to all the bad songs on the radio. Both when he loved me and when he didn't.

—Jenny Offill, *Dept. of Speculation*

There was a tacit understanding between them
that "liquor helped"; growing more miserable with
every glass one hoped for the moment of relief.

—Graham Greene, *The Heart of the Matter*

THE MOST PAINFUL THING IS LOSING YOURSELF IN THE PROCESS OF LOVING SOMEONE TOO MUCH, AND FORGETTING THAT YOU ARE SPECIAL TOO.

—Ernest Hemingway, *Men Without Women*

We can never go back again, that much is certain. The past is still close to us. The things we have tried to forget and put behind us would stir again, and that sense of fear, of furtive unrest, struggling at length to blind unreasoning panic—now mercifully stilled, thank God—might in some manner unforeseen become a living companion as it had before.

—Daphne du Maurier, *Rebecca*

The belief in a supernatural source
of evil is not necessary; men alone are
quite capable of every wickedness.

—Joseph Conrad, *Heart of Darkness*

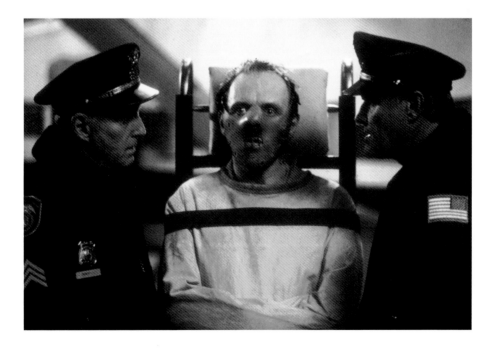

ANYBODY WHO HAS SURVIVED HIS CHILDHOOD HAS ENOUGH INFORMATION ABOUT LIFE TO LAST HIM THE REST OF HIS DAYS.

—Flannery O'Connor, *Mystery and Manners: Occasional Prose*

The place had filled him with a sense of wisdom hovering just out of reach, of unspeakable grace prepared and waiting just around the corner, but he'd walked himself weak down its endless blue streets and all the people who knew how to live had kept their tantalizing secret to themselves.

—Richard Yates, *Revolutionary Road*

The abiding American myth of the self-made man comes attached to another article of faith—an insistence, even—that every self-made man can sustain whatever self he has managed to make. A man divided—thwarting or interrupting his own mechanisms of survival—fails to sustain this myth, disrupts our belief in the absolute efficacy of willpower, and in these failures often forfeits his right to our sympathy. Or so the logic goes. But I wonder why this fractured self shouldn't warrant our compassion just as much as the self besieged? Or maybe even more?

—Leslie Jamison, *The Empathy Exams*

The world represented an endless sequence of celebrities replacing celebrities, like cheap wooden nesting dolls, each bearing a tinier and less persuasive likeness than the one that had come before.

—Kevin Brockmeier, *The Illumination*

Nothing, of course, will ever take the place of the good old fashion of "liking" a work of art or not liking it; the more improved criticism will not abolish that primitive, that ultimate, test.

—Henry James, *The Art of Fiction*

There are moments in life when it is all turned inside out—what is real becomes unreal, what is unreal becomes tangible, and all your levelheaded efforts to keep a tight ontological control are rendered silly and indulgent.

—Aleksandar Hemon, *The Lazarus Project*

PERHAPS ALL ROMANCE IS LIKE THAT; NOT A CONTRACT BETWEEN EQUAL PARTIES BUT AN EXPLOSION OF DREAMS AND DESIRES THAT CAN FIND NO OUTLET IN EVERYDAY LIFE. ONLY A DRAMA WILL DO AND WHILE THE FIREWORKS LAST THE SKY IS A DIFFERENT COLOR.

—Jeanette Winterson, *The Passion*

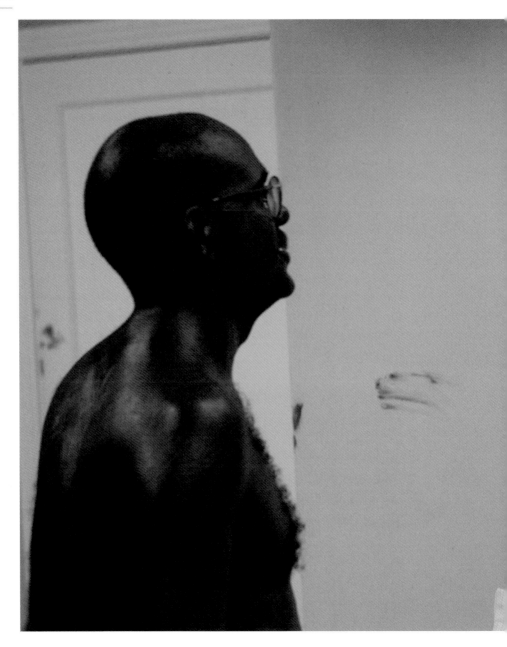

You meet people in your family you'd never happen to run into otherwise.

—Deborah Eisenberg,
*Twilight of the
Superheroes*

It was possible to feel superior to other people and feel like a misfit at the same time.

—Jeffrey Eugenides, *The Marriage Plot*

Like true friends, they take no hardy or elegant stance loosely choreographed from some broad perspective. They get right in there and mutter "Jesus Christ!" and shake their heads.

—Lorrie Moore, *Birds of America*

She did what girls generally do when they don't
feel the part: she dressed it instead.

—Zadie Smith, *On Beauty*

IT IS QUITE IMPOSSIBLE
THESE DAYS TO ASSUME
ANYTHING ABOUT PEOPLE'S
EDUCATIONAL LEVEL FROM
THE WAY THEY TALK OR
DRESS OR FROM THEIR
TASTE IN MUSIC. SAFEST
TO TREAT EVERYONE YOU
MEET AS A DISTINGUISHED
INTELLECTUAL.

—Ian McEwan, *Atonement*

The sense of unhappiness
is so much easier to convey
than that of happiness. In
misery we seem aware of our
own existence, even though
it may be in the form of a
monstrous egotism: this pain
of mine is individual, this
nerve that winces belongs
to me and to no other. But
happiness annihilates us: we
lose our identity.

—Graham Greene, *The End of
the Affair*

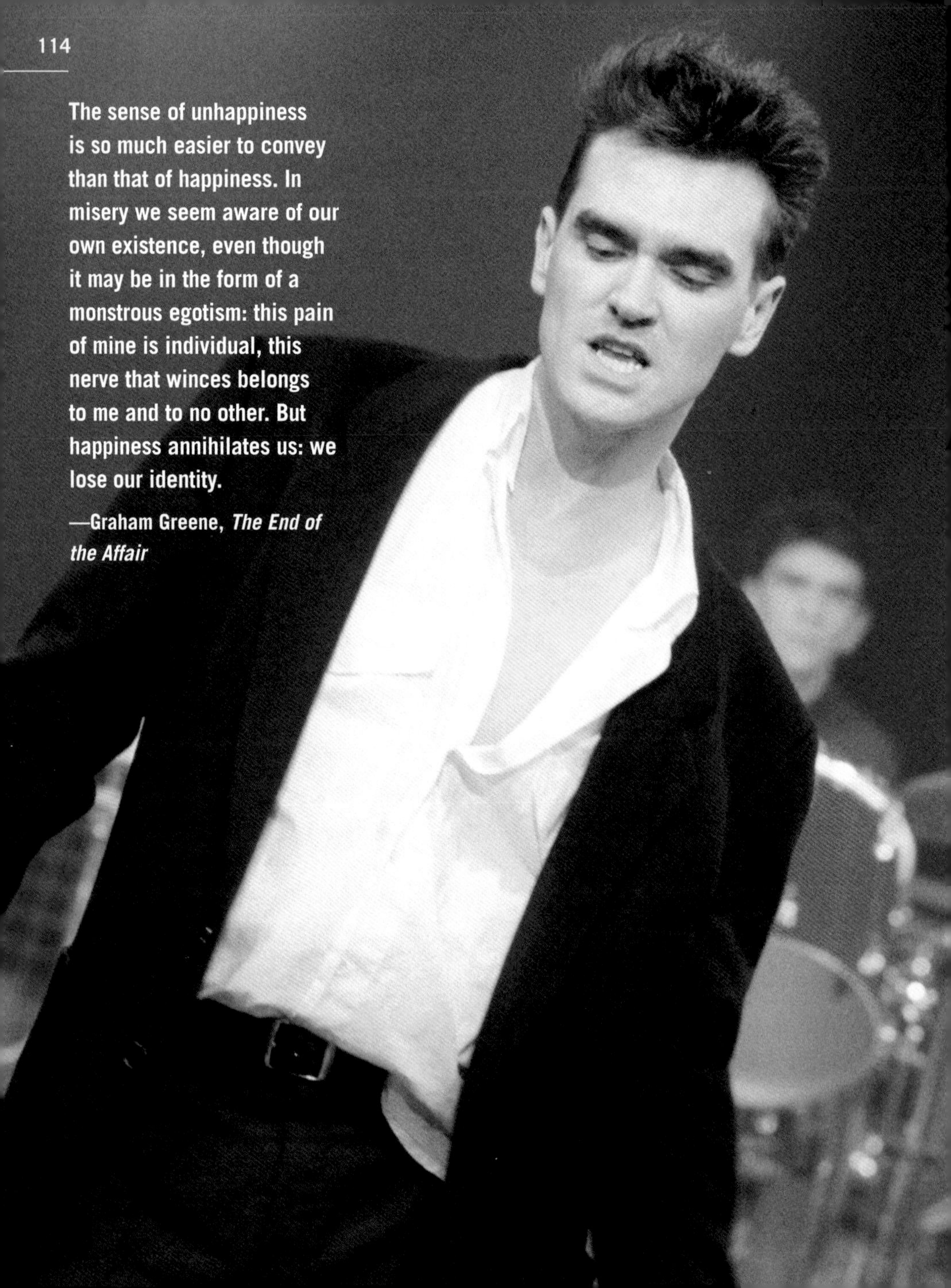

There could have been no two hearts so open,
no tastes so similar, no feelings so in unison.

—Jane Austen, *Persuasion*

Not giving a shit, she decided, is like the defrost option
on a car's heater that miraculously unfogs the windshield,
allowing you to see where you're headed.

—Richard Russo, *Empire Falls*

She could not explain or quite understand that it wasn't altogether jealousy she felt, it was rage. And not because she couldn't shop like that or dress like that. It was because that was what girls were supposed to be like. That was what men— people, everybody—thought they should be like. Beautiful, treasured, spoiled, selfish, pea-brained.

—Alice Munro, *Runaway*

To say a person is a happy person or an unhappy person is
ridiculous. We are a thousand different kinds of people every hour.

—Anthony Doerr, *Memory Wall*

We are, all four of us, blood relatives, and we speak a kind of esoteric, family language, a sort of semantic geometry in which the shortest distance between any two points is a fullish circle.

—J. D. Salinger, *Franny and Zooey*

Perhaps one never seems so much at one's ease as when one has to play a part.

—Oscar Wilde, *The Picture of Dorian Gray*

Many farcical, illogical, incom-
prehensible transactions are
subsumed by the mania of lust.
—Philip Roth, *Sabbath's Theater*

Some people are reference works of their own obsessions and desires, constantly cross-indexed and brimming with information. They do not wait to be consulted, they just supply.

—Elizabeth McCracken,
The Giant's House

I WANT TO JUST BE LAZY AND I WANT SOME OF THE PEOPLE AROUND ME TO BE DOING THINGS, BECAUSE THAT MAKES ME FEEL COMFORTABLE AND SAFE—AND I WANT SOME OF THEM TO BE DOING NOTHING AT ALL, BECAUSE THEY CAN BE GRACEFUL AND COMPANIONABLE FOR ME.

—F. Scott Fitzgerald, *The Beautiful and Damned*

I was not ladylike, nor was I manly. I was something else altogether. There were so many different ways to be beautiful.

—Michael Cunningham, *A Home at the End of the World*

I often felt the girls' speech was interchangeable, without any individuality whatsoever, a kind of herd-speak they had all agreed upon.

—Siri Hustvedt, *The Summer Without Men*

I think certain types of processes don't allow for any variation. If you have to be part of that process, all you can do is transform—or perhaps distort—yourself through that persistent repetition, and make that process a part of your own personality.

—Haruki Murakami, *What I Talk About When I Talk About Running*

The only relationship that can make both partners happy is one in which sentimentality has no place and neither partner makes any claim on the life and freedom of the other.

—Milan Kundera, *The Unbearable Lightness of Being*

For madness is seductive, sexy.
Female madness. So long as the female
is reasonably young and attractive.

—Joyce Carol Oates, *Blonde*

When small towns find they cannot harm the strangest of their members, when eccentrics show resilience, they are eventually embraced and even cherished.

—Louise Erdrich, *The Master Butchers Singing Club*

He had to have her, he definitely had to have her. She was not merely the latest object on which his greedy desire to be saved had fixed itself; no, she was the woman who was going to save him. The woman whose fine intelligence and deep sympathy and divine body, yes, whose divine body would successfully deflect his attention from the gloomy well shaft of his feelings and the contemplation of his past.

—Edward St. Aubyn, *Bad News*

In this instant, shaken to her very depths, this ecstatic human being has a first inkling that the soul is made of stuff so mysteriously elastic that a single event can make it big enough to contain the infinite.

—Stefan Zweig, *The Post-Office Girl*

He'd once told me that the art of getting ahead in New York was based on learning how to express dissatisfaction in an interesting way. The air was full of rage and complaint. People had no tolerance for your particular hardship unless you knew how to entertain them with it.

—Don DeLillo, *White Noise*

The years of illusion aren't those of adolescence, as the grown-ups try to tell us; they're the ones immediately after it, say the middle twenties, the false maturity if you like, when you first get thoroughly embroiled in things and lose your head.

—Kingsley Amis, *Lucky Jim*

If you asked me now who I am, the only answer I could give with any certainty would be my name. For the rest: my loves, my hates, down even to my deepest desires, I can no longer say whether these emotions are my own, or stolen from those I once so desperately wished to be.

—Evelyn Waugh, *Brideshead Revisited*

IN TRUTH, THERE ARE ONLY TWO REALITIES: THE ONE FOR PEOPLE WHO ARE IN LOVE OR LOVE EACH OTHER, AND THE ONE FOR PEOPLE WHO ARE STANDING OUTSIDE ALL THAT.

—Charles Baxter, The Feast of Love

And the little screaming fact that sounds through all history: repression works only to strengthen and knit the repressed.

—John Steinbeck, *The Grapes of Wrath*

We have such numerous interests in our lives that it is not uncommon, on a single occasion, for the foundations of a happiness that does not yet exist to be laid down alongside the intensification of a grief from which we are still suffering.

—Marcel Proust, *Swann's Way*

A shared passion for a subject, large or small, could quickly put two strangers into a special state of subdued rapture and rivalry, distantly resembling love; but you had to hit on the subject.

—Alan Hollinghurst, *The Line of Beauty*

TO LIVE IN METROPOLIS WAS TO KNOW THAT THE EXCEPTIONAL WAS AS COMMONPLACE AS DIET SODA, THAT ABNORMALITY WAS THE POPCORN NORM.

—Salman Rushdie, *Fury*

There are occasions when a woman, no matter how weak and impotent in character she may be in comparison with a man, will yet suddenly become not only harder than any man, but even harder than anything and everything in the world.

—Nikolai Gogol, *Dead Souls*

MAYBE TIMES ARE NEVER STRANGE TO WOMEN: IT IS JUST ONE CONTINUOUS MONOTONOUS THING FULL OF THE REPEATED FOLLIES OF THEIR MENFOLKS.

—William Faulkner, *The Unvanquished*

Perhaps this is what we mean by sanity: that, whatever our self-admitted eccentricities might be, we are not villains of our own stories.

—Teju Cole, *Open City*

MY LIFE IS SPENT IN ONE LONG EFFORT TO ESCAPE
FROM THE COMMONPLACES OF EXISTENCE.
THESE LITTLE PROBLEMS HELP ME TO DO SO.

—Arthur Conan Doyle, "The Red-Headed League"

Is it because we're having so much fun at home we've forgotten the world? Is it because we're so rich and the rest of the world's so poor and we just don't care if they are? I've heard rumors; the world is starving, but we're well fed. Is it true, the world works hard and we play? Is that why we're hated so much?

—Ray Bradbury, *Fahrenheit 451*

How soon country people forget. When they fall in love with a city it is forever, and it is like forever. As though there never was a time when they didn't love it. The minute they arrive at the train station or get off the ferry and glimpse the wide streets and the wasteful lamps lighting them, they know they are born for it. There, in a city, they are not so much new as themselves: their stronger, riskier selves.

—Toni Morrison, *Jazz*

To paraphrase several sages: Nobody can think and hit someone at the same time.

—Susan Sontag, *Regarding the Pain of Others*

We don't know what
we'd do. Nobody
knows what accident
of fate or DNA
or character will
determine how we
act when the shit
hits the fan.

—Francine Prose,
Guided Tours of Hell

I know that's what people say—you'll get over it. I'd say it, too. But I know it's not true. Oh, you'll be happy again, never fear. But you won't forget. Every time you fall in love it will be because something in the man reminds you of him.

—Betty Smith, *A Tree Grows in Brooklyn*

Loving humanity means as much and as little as loving raindrops, or loving the Milky Way. You say that you love humanity? Are you sure you aren't treating yourself to easy self-congratulation, seeking approval, making certain you're on the right side?

—Julian Barnes, *Flaubert's Parrot*

Without even realizing it he'd fallen into one of those Let's Be Friends vortexes, the bane of nerdboys everywhere. These relationships were love's version of a stay in the stocks, in you go, plenty of misery guaranteed and what you got out of it besides bitterness and heartbreak nobody knows. Perhaps some knowledge of self and women.

—Junot Díaz, *The Brief Wondrous Life of Oscar Wao*

It now lately sometimes seemed a black miracle to me that people could actually care deeply about a subject or pursuit, and could go on caring this way for years on end. Could dedicate their entire lives to it. It seemed admirable and at the same time pathetic. We are all dying to give our lives away to something, maybe.

—David Foster Wallace, *Infinite Jest*

Perhaps it's that you can't go back in time, but you can return to the scenes of a love, of a crime, of happiness, and of a fatal decision; the places are what remain, are what you can possess, are what is immortal. They become the tangible landscape of memory, the places that made you, and in some way you too become them.

—Rebecca Solnit, *A Field Guide to Getting Lost*

NO EVIL DOOMS
US HOPELESSLY
EXCEPT THE EVIL WE
LOVE, AND DESIRE
TO CONTINUE IN, AND
MAKE NO EFFORT TO
ESCAPE FROM.

—George Eliot, *Daniel Deronda*

There are innumerable marriages where two people, both twisted and wrong in their depths, are well matched, making each other miserable in the way they need, in the way the pattern of their life demands.

—Doris Lessing, *The Grass Is Singing*

He looked at her neck and thought how he would like to jab it with the knife he had for his muffin. He knew enough anatomy to make pretty certain of getting the carotid artery. And at the same time he wanted to cover her pale, thin face with kisses.

—W. Somerset Maugham, *Of Human Bondage*

There's a fine line between thinking about somebody and thinking about not thinking about somebody, but I have the patience and the self-control to walk that line for hours—days, if I have to.

—Jennifer Egan, *A Visit from the Goon Squad*

APPENDIX

Chinua Achebe / *Girls* (19) Perhaps no TV character symbolizes first-world problems and the phenomenon of the "white whine" better than Hannah Horvath. The first episode of Lena Dunham's HBO comedy, *Girls*, depicts the horror of recent college grad Hannah when her parents cut her off and refuse to subsidize her Brooklyn apartment rent any longer. This is a tragedy of epic proportions to jobless, aimless Hannah. The show launched a zillion Internet think pieces about the tunnel vision that unearned privilege affords, but Nigerian novelist Chinua Achebe's essay collection *Hopes and Impediments*, published in 1988, is still a defining piece of work on the subject.

Kingsley Amis / *Friends* (134) Kingsley Amis's 1954 debut, *Lucky Jim*, is frequently called out as one of the funniest novels of the twentieth century—it's a mishmash of drunken misunderstandings and small-level scandals that afflict an aspiring young lecturer. The '90s sitcom *Friends* is similarly hilarious, if not nearly as academic in subject matter. In showing the trials and tribulations of a group of postcollegiates trying on the trappings of adulthood, *Friends* became a cultural phenomenon and inspired more than a few "Rachel" hairdos.

Maya Angelou / Bruce Springsteen (61) In Maya Angelou's 2009 collection of essays written to the daughter she never had, the poet talks about the lasting impact that one's home can have throughout one's life. It's unsurprising, then, that blue-collar poet Bruce Springsteen shares these sentiments, that Springsteen's idea of home is both a place from which so many of the heroes of his songs yearn to flee and something to be celebrated. For all his talk of "death traps" and factory closings, Springsteen is an active advocate for his New Jersey hometown and a hero to his neighbors.

 Margaret Atwood / *Game of Thrones* (69) Spoiler alert: Season three's Red Wedding episode caught many viewers off guard, and reminded us to never get too comfortable when watching HBO's *Game of Thrones*. In Margaret Atwood's 2000 Booker Prize–winning novel, *The Blind Assassin*, a woman attempts to dissect the events that surround the mysterious death of her sister, a disaster that leaves her reeling more profoundly than even the most invested *Game of Thrones* fan.

 Margaret Atwood / *The Golden Girls* (56) On Saturday nights in the 1980s NBC viewers of all ages had the pleasure of finding out that a quartet of Florida retirees could be incredibly entertaining. How fun it was to watch the antics of Dorothy, Blanche, Rose, and Sophia and realize that they were as silly as we were—how revelatory that comedy could so thoroughly break generational boundaries. Margaret Atwood breaks boundaries by writing about rivalries and bonds between women in ways that are intrinsically relatable no matter her heroines' ages or how realistic or fantastical the worlds they inhabit.

 Jane Austen / *Wayne's World* (115) It's a relationship worthy of a Jane Austen romance, one in which the couple in question is so like-minded that they seem destined for a happy ending. The 1992 comedy *Wayne's World*, based on the popular *Saturday Night Live* skit, follows the adventures of Wayne Campbell and his sidekick Garth Algar (Mike Myers and Dana Carvey) as they host a cable-access show on which they share an enthusiasm for girls and music and all the things that make them say "Schwing!" an awful lot. Wayne and Garth are proof that "Party on!" can be a cry of comradeship and that best friendship can be its own form of true love.

Paul Auster / *There's Something About Mary* (28) Paul Auster's 1989 novel, *Moon Palace*, is the story of three generations of one American family and their many cyclical coincidences and overlaps—many as charming as *There's Something About Mary*, but few nearly as gross. The Farrelly brothers' 1998 romantic comedy stars Cameron Diaz as the all-too-trusting dream girl next door who inspires all kinds of depravity in the men who adore her (there are many, including former QB Brett Favre). Ben Stiller plays Ted, a suitor who's been crushing on Mary since grade school, and in an infamous scene, he accidentally shares his "hair gel" with Mary. She confidently applies it, and the rest is sight gag history.

 John Banville / *The Goonies* (34) In 1985 a bunch of kids discover a secret treasure map and set off to follow it and have all kinds of adventures. *The Goonies* is nothing but good fun, in part because—spoiler alert—it has an unambiguously happy ending. In John Banville's Booker Prize–winning 2005 novel, *The Sea*, a grieving man returns to the Irish seaside village of his childhood for some instant nostalgia, the way some of us rewatch *The Goonies* over and over.

 Julian Barnes / Bono (151) There came a point in the long career of U2's front man, Bono, when his political activism began to seem more like a pretentious marketing tool than a humanitarian calling. In one of his most off-putting "it's all about me" moments, the Irish musician and enormously successful private equity financier became one of the leading spokespeople about the death of South African president Nelson Mandela and the importance of his legacy. In Julian Barnes's 1984 novel, *Flaubert's Parrot*, an aspiring expert on Gustave Flaubert answers accusations that the French author hated humanity by arguing that loving a specific few is better than loving all, a concept that is clearly foreign to the holier-than-thou rock star.

Julian Barnes / Kurt Cobain and Courtney Love (16) It's hard to look back on photos of Kurt Cobain and Courtney Love and not feel a tragic sense of loss, but for a moment in the '90s they were the king and queen of the grunge rock movement that defined the decade. Their reign as a couple was brief, but their legacy has been long lasting. The protagonist of Julian Barnes's short novel *The Sense of an Ending* is a middle-aged man looking back on haunting events from his young adulthood—namely a relationship gone sour and the suicide of a close friend. It's a novel concerned with the beauty of the most fleeting moments.

 Charles Baxter / Brad Pitt and Angelina Jolie (136) In Charles Baxter's 2000 novel, *The Feast of Love*, a coffee shop owner who takes note of the dramas of his customers' daily lives acknowledges that the narrative we create for those we observe is its own kind of truth. Never were Baxter's narrator's sentiments more poignant than in 2005 when Brad Pitt split from Jennifer Aniston and he and Angelina Jolie officially became known as Brangelina. This resulted in a virtual civil war of *Us Weekly* readers—you were either solidly on Team Jen or Team Angie; there was no room for maybes. In the ensuing years the couple has raised a bunch of children and starred in many films and gotten married, but speculation about the health of their relationship is still a favorite topic among tabloid writers and readers alike.

 Jo Ann Beard / *Bob's Burgers* (41) "Time for the charm bomb to explode," says Tina Belcher monotonously, with a flip of her blocky black hair. The eldest child on FOX's hit animated series *Bob's Burgers* wields a weird and wonderful confidence that belies her awkward preteen image. Jo Ann Beard's 2011 novel, *In Zanesville*, captures the special power of a particular kind of late bloomer, those gawky young girls who might not always command the spotlight but who have a special glow just the same.

Aimee Bender / *The Simpsons* (25) Homer and Bart Simpson have perhaps a more intense love-hate relationship than almost any other two characters on television. That they're father and son makes their sparring endearing; that they're cartoons makes the violence of their encounters seem less like a case for child protective services. Aimee Bender's 2010 novel, *The Particular Sadness of Lemon Cake*, contains some whimsy and a bit of magical realism, but mostly it delineates what it's like when a child begins to understand that her parents are, after all, only human.

 Ray Bradbury / Paris and Nicky Hilton (146) Who better to represent the dystopian world of Ray Bradbury's most celebrated novel than Paris and Nicky Hilton? In the early aughts the hotel heiress siblings were symbols of vapid baby-pink-colored excess; their wealth and fame and anti-intellectualism were fetishized by tabloid mags and reality shows alike.

 Kevin Brockmeier / *Keeping Up with the Kardashians* (104) The members of the Kardashian clan have come to represent a new kind of celebrity culture, a culture in which fame and riches don't necessarily come as results of having talent—or at least not the kind of talent for which they give out awards. If Kim is the grand dame of the Kardashians, her siblings are perhaps more like the nesting dolls that Kevin Brockmeier describes in his 2011 novel in which internal pain becomes visible and beautiful, and the world must learn to interact on a deeper, less superficial level.

 A. S. Byatt / *The Notebook* (3) A. S. Byatt's 1990 Booker Prize–winning novel, *Possession*, is a literary mystery that incidentally solves the riddle of why the film adaptation of a cheesy Nicholas Sparks novel can feel profound. Sometimes an old-fashioned genre romance can be incredibly satisfying because of its conventions, especially when it comes with a shirtless Ryan Gosling.

Truman Capote / *The Shining* (39) All of the small details in Truman Capote's 1966 true crime novel about the murder of a midwestern family may not be 100 percent correct, but the book itself is so artfully written that the mood is always right. It's not 100 percent clear whether the beleaguered writer Jack Torrance in Stanley Kubrick's 1980 horror film based on Stephen King's 1977 novel is haunted by actual ghosts or by madness, but it doesn't seem to matter: the end result is horrifying either way.

Michael Chabon / *Harold & Kumar Go to White Castle* (51) In which the search for fast food by a couple of stoners becomes an epic quest. The 2004 comedy *Harold & Kumar Go to White Castle*, starring John Cho and Kal Penn, is as high concept as its title suggests, with a simple trip for burgers turning into a story worthy of Don Quixote and Sancho Panza. Michael Chabon's 1995 novel about a struggling novelist who seems to smoke weed more than he actually writes, and the editor who comes to check up on him and ends up having a few quixotic quests of his own, evokes Cervantes's literary masterpiece to capture that same sense of juvenile goadings among guy friends.

Dan Chaon / Lindsay Lohan (14) Anyone who saw the films of Lindsay Lohan's earlier career knew she had "it," that special spark that befits a movie star. However, Lilo's mug shots and photos of her passed out in a car now might be just as, if not more, familiar than images from *Freaky Friday*. In Dan Chaon's story "Prodigal" from his collection *Among the Missing*, a son reflects on how all of his father's worst qualities have become defining characteristics of their troubled relationship. Whether it's fair or not, it aptly illustrates the sentiment that our best work can be obscured by our weakest moments.

Teju Cole / *Pirates of the Caribbean* **(144)** Credit a megasuccessful film franchise based on a Disney ride for introducing the concept of the rock-and-roll pirate. As played by Johnny Depp, hero Jack Sparrow is Keith Richards in pirate form, meaning that he has heavily lined eyes and acts kookily and is seemingly always drunk but witty. In Teju Cole's 2011 novel, *Open City*, a Nigerian psychology student walks around New York City and makes plenty of observations about the people he sees. Given that the story is told from his point of view, the novel's narrator will always be the hero, despite the revelation of his many flaws, just as Sparrow is endowed with too many leading-man charms to be a true bad guy.

 Joseph Conrad / *The Silence of the Lambs* **(95)** "I ate his liver with some fava beans and a nice Chianti." Hannibal Lecter is a good place to start if we need proof that men are scarier than monsters. Cannibalism is also a major theme in Joseph Conrad's *Heart of Darkness*, an 1899 novel set along the ivory trading routes in Africa in which the line between civility and barbarity is blurry, at best. Here's a hint, Clarisse: The white imperialists are much more terrifying than any other characters in the book, including the cannibals.

 Michael Cunningham / Prince (125) Michael Cunningham's novels are filled with well-drawn, multidimensional characters, some of whom don't easily fit into any traditional gender roles. Prince Rogers Nelson—known to us by his first name only—oozes sexuality with every song he sings, every guitar solo he whales, and every high note he hits. His androgynous appeal reached its apex in his 1984 rock opera, *Purple Rain*, a film and an album in which he mixes and blends musical genres to great effect. The Purple One, just like so many Michael Cunningham characters, flays traditional notions about gender and sexuality, and the world is a better place for it.

Lydia Davis / *Louie* (62) Neurosis and self-loathing are traits that can be found in a wide, wide array of stand-up comedians, but very few are as engaging and charming as Louis CK. On his FX comedy he portrays a version of himself who is incessantly observant about the world in general and aware of his own flaws in particular, but who is also given to flights of fancy. The title character in Lydia Davis's story "The Professor," which ran in *Harper's* in 1992 and was later anthologized in a 1997 collection, is stuck in her own head and desperately needs an escape. She therefore daydreams about falling in love with a cowboy, an impractical desire that would make for a great fantasy sequence on *Louie*.

 Don DeLillo / *Seinfeld* (133) Cosmo Kramer, Jerry's irrepressible neighbor on the classic '90s sitcom *Seinfeld*, is known for his vintage shirts and his zany hair and his ability to get worked up into a frenzy over a wide variety of silly things. He's never ever afraid to say exactly what's on his mind at any time, and his lack of filter is exactly the kind of aggression so heavily celebrated by the head of the pop culture department at a midwestern liberal arts college in Don DeLillo's 1985 breakout novel, *White Noise*, a man who processes most human behavior through the lens of entertainment.

 Junot Díaz / *Pretty in Pink* (152) The term "friend zone" could have been created specifically for Duckie (Jon Cryer), the well-meaning goof who is hopelessly in love with his best friend, Andie (Molly Ringwald), in John Hughes's 1986 comedy classic, *Pretty in Pink*. The poor guy doesn't stand a chance, especially when rich and charming Blane (Andrew McCarthy) comes along. The title character of Junot Díaz's 2007 novel is a self-aware comic book nerd who understands the plight of guys like himself and Duckie, even as his narration makes him more compelling than a guy like Blane could ever be.

Charles Dickens / *South Park: Bigger, Longer & Uncut* **(37)** Matt Stone and Trey Parker's big-screen version of their Comedy Central cartoon evokes major Dickensian themes of social injustice, while also containing a large variety of imaginative swear words that couldn't be said on cable TV. After Kenny, Cartman, Kyle, and Stan see their favorite Canadian duo, Terrance and Phillip, in a new R-rated movie, they can't stop cursing gleefully. When their parents want the United States to invade Canada in retaliation for all that filthiness, the kids of South Park band together with a common cause, having a full-on *Les Miz* moment (the Broadway musical, not Victor Hugo's book!) with lots of inspiring singing and the promise of revolution.

 Joan Didion / **Taylor Swift (5)** Fifty years before Taylor Swift became the tearstained breakup goddess of the pop-country music scene, Joan Didion wrote a scathing description of folk singer Joan Baez in *Slouching Towards Bethlehem*. Didion characterizes Baez as the wide-eyed mascot of the 1960s—a singer who's more persona than person. Even if Tay sings more about romantic travails with movie stars than she does about war protests, Didion zeroes in on a quality—*feeling things*—that pinpoints the appeal of both wide-eyed pop stars.

 Anthony Doerr / *Alias* **(118)** J. J. Abrams's early aughts TV series stars Jennifer Garner as Sydney Bristow, a CIA spy whose job requires her to change her wardrobe, hair color, and personality with alarming regularity. Anthony Doerr's story anthologized in his 2010 collection of the same name, *Memory Wall*, is the tale of an older woman who suffers from memory loss and undergoes a procedure allowing her to extract her memories and watch them on her wall like a film, seeing so many different versions of herself flashing by.

Fyodor Dostoyevsky / *My So-Called Life* (9) For one brief season in the mid-'90s, the girls' bathroom at Liberty High School was the coolest place to be. *My So-Called Life* captures coming of age like no other show, and Rayanne Graff is the impossibly cool girl who seems to have it all figured out. And yet her world-weary ways belie her vulnerability, a condition that aligns her with some of the great characters from Russian literature.

 Fyodor Dostoyevsky / *The Wire* (53) Dostoyevsky's *The Brothers Karamazov* is a touchstone of Russian literature when it comes to tackling huge philosophical questions of morality and ethics. HBO's groundbreaking drama *The Wire* might just be the TV equivalent of Dostoyevsky's great epics. The show explores the drug wars in the streets of Baltimore from a variety of angles, but one of the most compelling is dealer Omar Little (Michael K. Williams), a complicated antihero who lives by his own moral code and often shows great tenderness in certain areas of his life even as he carries out hits on the streets.

 Arthur Conan Doyle / *Indiana Jones and the Temple of Doom* (145) Indiana Jones has the most exciting life of any archaeologist in the history of the profession. He's always off on some romp, and it's a great escapist pleasure to join in the fun by watching him, even when his adventures involve his most hated enemy: snakes. Similarly, Sir Arthur Conan Doyle's most famous hero solves mysteries as a means to escape the drudgery of everyday life, although Sherlock Holmes's methods are often more cerebral— and less dirty—than Indy's.

 Daphne du Maurier / *Pretty Little Liars* (98) Daphne du Maurier was a master of setting a creepy mood with literary prowess as she plotted page-turners like *Rebecca*, in which a young woman is tormented by the specter of her new husband's first wife. An ABC Family nighttime drama uses a similar formula to tell the story of a group of cool teenage girls haunted—literally?—by the ghost of an old frenemy. As amusingly far-fetched as it tends to become, *Pretty Little Liars* somehow manages to maintain an atmosphere of drama with the suspense of knowing that some horrific disaster could be just a text message away.

David James Duncan / Tom Cruise (48) David James Duncan's epic 1992 novel, *The Brothers K*, explores the world of Seventh Day Adventists, and the delusions he describes that so often accompany religious epiphanies ring eerily similar to Tom Cruise's behavior during his infamous 2005 appearance on *The Oprah Winfrey Show*. Was his creepily exuberant performance staged, or was it all utterly sincere? Either way, it was bonkers. When he leapt onto Oprah's couch with a wild look in his eyes to announce his undying love for actress Katie Holmes, Cruise's movie star cred began to slip away, and he became the butt of many a joke. Seemingly unfazed and still mega-intense, he reenacted the *Oprah* moment shortly after with Jay Leno on *The Tonight Show*.

Elaine Dundy / *NSYNC (13) The narrator of Elaine Dundy's delight-ful 1958 novel, *The Dud Avocado*, about the adventures of a young American girl in Paris, notices a trend among expats that very well applies to boy bands, past and present. Take, for instance, *NSYNC's 2000 tour, and see how their images—"the sensitive one," "the one with the funny hair," "the player"—all blend together.

Katherine Dunn / *House of Cards* (84) To compare the machinations of US politics to a circus is a well-worn metaphor, but Netflix's original series *House of Cards* does a particularly great job of revealing exactly how much Washington, DC, relies on smoke and mirrors. As played by Kevin Spacey, Frank Underwood is a corrupt politician who lies and cheats to get what he wants, all while smiling for the camera. In Katherine

Dunn's 1989 novel, *Geek Love*, set in the world of a traveling carnival, a circus performer turned cult leader acknowledges the appeal of false beliefs—without them it would be abundantly clear that the whole world is a freak show.

 Jennifer Egan / *My So-Called Life* (159) No teenager can overthink quite as brilliantly as Angela Chase can. Her voice-overs give each episode of *My So-Called Life* a window into her philosophies and fixations, mostly involving her crush on dreamy high school bad boy Jordan Catalano. Jennifer Egan's 2010 novel takes obsession to a much less adorable space: the rambling thoughts of an East River fisherman who has a very important meeting with a record exec. *A Visit from the Goon Squad* shifts perspectives with every chapter, reminding readers that everyone we encounter has his own Angela Chase–like narrative running through his head.

 Deborah Eisenberg / *Arrested Development* (108) "Now the story of a wealthy family who lost everything and the one son who had no choice but to keep them all together." In the FOX sitcom *Arrested Development* Jason Bateman plays Michael Bluth, the ultimate straight man, who must deal with his wacky family, including his brother-in-law, Tobias Fünke, who regularly blues himself with paint just in case the Blue Man Group ever needs a stand-in. Deborah Eisenberg is a master of short stories that contain a dark sense of humor and an eye for revealing the absurdity of everyday life, which the Bluth family is more than able to illustrate.

 George Eliot / *Breaking Bad* (156) Intention matters, suggests Daniel Deronda, the title hero of George Eliot's last published novel. *Breaking Bad*'s antihero Walter White has medical bills to pay and a family to support, so at first putting his skills as a chemist to work by cooking up some blue meth to sell seems like an almost noble plan. But the show's impressive run on AMC follows the evolution of Walt from average guy to supervillain. We see the utter pleasure he takes in the power he acquires as a drug kingpin, and that beneath his black fedora and dark sunglasses lies a monster with motives that are anything but virtuous.

George Eliot / *The Sopranos* (2) Tony Soprano is one of TV's most compelling main characters of all time because he contains multitudes: He's the ruthless head of a violent New Jersey crime family who also happens to have panic attacks and mommy issues and can, at times, be a sentimental sap who's capable of great warmth and affection—especially for his children. Just as George Eliot's masterpiece *Middlemarch* features a cast of multidimensional and nuanced characters, so too does *The Sopranos*, the HBO series that reminds us that mob bosses have feelings too.

Ralph Ellison / *Hedwig and the Angry Inch* (75) *Invisible Man*, Ralph Ellison's 1952 novel about a black man who feels unseen in America's racist and divided society, ends with his protagonist forced literally to go underground. John Cameron Mitchell's rock opera, *Hedwig and the Angry Inch*, features a transgendered East German singer who is as lonely and wrathful as Ellison's invisible man—she and her band are "internationally ignored" despite costuming and catchy music that beg to be noticed.

Ralph Waldo Emerson / Clint Eastwood (46) The transcendentalist Emerson warned that great men tend to wither with time, and yes, watching Clint Eastwood address an empty chair meant to stand in for President Obama was as anticlimactic as *Dirty Harry* was heart-racing.

Louise Erdrich / *Twin Peaks* (130) "My log has something to tell you." The Log Lady is an institution in the small Washington town of Twin Peaks, and one of the groundbreaking crime drama's great mysteries is whether the log she carries around with her everywhere has true clairvoyant powers and the ability to warn others about dangers ahead, or if it is simply a piece of wood. Louise Erdrich's *The Master Butchers Singing Club* is a novel that depicts life in a small town in North Dakota, and the ways in which the residents come to celebrate its weirdos.

 Jeffrey Eugenides / *Daria* (110) It's a blessing and a curse for Daria Morgendorffer that she's smarter than everyone at Lawndale High School, including her teachers. The title character of the late '90s MTV series has some choice sarcastic words for just about everything, and the world is a better place for it—she is a master observer and an outsider, both. Jeffrey Eugenides's 2011 novel, *The Marriage Plot*, is a lovely study of Brown University characters who are academically advanced but still not entirely socially adept.

 William Faulkner / *Game of Thrones* (142) William Faulkner and George R. R. Martin are quite the duo if you're looking for a sweaty combination of violence and machismo. But both Faulkner, in his 1938 Civil War novel, *The Unvanquished*, and Martin, in the HBO series based on his best-selling books, acknowledge the roles women play in the violent worlds they've built. Daenerys Targaryen (Amelia Clarke) might be *Game of Thrones*'s biggest hero of all, a woman who takes control of her husband's Dothraki army after his death and rules with great moral strength, severe intolerance for any bullshit, and three dragons for children.

 F. Scott Fitzgerald / *Girls* (124) Lena Dunham has made extraordinary accomplishments as a writer, actress, and director, but her TV alter ego is not similarly motivated. Eighty years before Hannah Horvath and her aimless friends moved to Brooklyn and made an art of underemployed ennui, F. Scott Fitzgerald wrote about a wealthy young Manhattan couple who also were not exactly career oriented. But the privilege of being able to just hang out with no particular goals or ambitions can be a curse, as Fitzgerald's doomed couple learns.

 F. Scott Fitzgerald / *Mad Men* (21) AMC's *Mad Men* is downright Fitzgeraldian in the way it combines glamour and elegance and tons of booze with existential despair. Joan Holloway is the show's resident redheaded bombshell, an enterprising woman who must work within the confines of 1960s mores and overtly sexist office culture in hopes of achieving her greater ambitions. As she struggles to find agency in her life and her career, she is unafraid to use her feminine allure to work her way up the corporate ladder, a strategy that is both undeniably denigrating and often quite effective.

 Gustave Flaubert / *Before Sunrise* (40) French novelist and playwright Gustave Flaubert broke new ground as both a realist and a romantic, capturing the small details of ordinary living along with a sense that emotional experiences heighten our everyday lives. Richard Linklater's 1995 film, *Before Sunrise*, stars Ethan Hawke and Julie Delpy as an American man and a French woman who meet in Vienna and have one night together to fall in love. Their relationship is constantly tinged by the knowledge that the clock is ticking down, and the film is shot over the course of this one intense night—a plot as realistic and romantic as it gets.

 Richard Ford / *The Big Lebowski* (65) The Coen brothers' 1998 comedy about a case of mistaken identity that spirals way out of control made a folk hero out of "the Dude," a very chill guy-cum-everyman hero played by Jeff Bridges. The Dude likes to hang out and smoke weed and drink White Russians, and he certainly never expects the guys on his bowling team to be dragged into his troubles. The desperately unhappy writer who is the subject of Richard Ford's 1996 novel, *The Sportswriter*, doesn't have a tight-knit bowling team to help him out when the shit hits the fan, but the members of his suburban Divorced Men's Club will have to do in a time of crisis.

 E. M. Forster / *Say Anything* . . . (87) E. M. Forster's 1908 novel, *A Room With a View*, follows a repressed young woman whose world begins to open up during a trip to Italy, where she falls for an unconventional young man of whom her strict family disapproves. Now cut to the romantic dramedy *Say Anything* in 1989, to Diane, a gorgeous brainy girl who works hard and plays a dutiful daughter to her difficult-to-please father, but who yearns for more. Cue Lloyd Dobler, a more or less average high school kid with an unexpected charisma. As played by John Cusack, Lloyd is unafraid to let the world know how crazy he is for Diane, and the moment when he blasts his boom box in her honor is a defining moment in their burgeoning relationship, and in '80s movies in general.

 Jonathan Franzen / Anna Nicole Smith (86) Poor doomed Anna Nicole Smith, the 1993 Playmate of the Year whose short life contained all the trappings of an *E! True Hollywood Story*—a wrong-side-of-the-tracks backstory, a tabloid-ready marriage to an elderly millionaire, a reality TV show, and a debilitating drug problem. Up until her death in 2007 the Marilyn Monroe look-alike was a symbol of the trials and tribulations associated with the darker sides of fame. Jonathan Franzen's 2001 breakout novel, *The Corrections*, contains an observation that a man makes about his elderly mother—how, through the course of their relationship, she has become more symbol than person to him. Sadly Anna Nicole contained a similar level of unknowability, so blinded were we all by the character she played.

 Mary Gaitskill / *Boogie Nights* (45) Paul Thomas Anderson's epic 1997 film about a rising (pun intended) porn actor starred Mark Wahlberg, who was previously best known for being the dude in the Calvin Klein underwear ads. Wahlberg plays Dirk Diggler (a screen name, naturally), a man who becomes known throughout the San Fernando Valley for his, um, bulging talents. Mary Gaitskill is known for her blisteringly honest depictions of sexuality told from a woman's point of view, but Dirk Diggler is a good reminder that sometimes it sucks for men to be objectified, too.

Gabriel García Márquez / *Gilmore Girls* (29) Only magical realism could explain how mom and daughter Lorelai and Rory Gilmore of the WB dramedy *Gilmore Girls* could manage to consume extravagant quantities of junk food while watching movies together at home on their couch and still look like models. In Gabriel García Márquez's 1985 novel, *Love in the Time of Cholera*, a woman overcomes her ambivalence about motherhood by befriending her son, just as Lorelai Gilmore is BFFs with her daughter, with whom she shares a coffee addiction, an inclination toward boy drama, and a near superhuman ability to inhale processed food.

William H. Gass / Lance Armstrong (63) William H. Gass writes the kind of difficult yet rewarding philosophical novel that you have to work really hard to read, and he worked nearly thirty years to write *The Tunnel*, finally published in 1995. Slow and steady. Lance Armstrong was a record-breaking cyclist, a Wheaties box cover model, a best-selling author, and a charity hero: his yellow Livestrong bracelets were de rigueur among athletic types, and all of the proceeds went to cancer patients. But the celebrated role model fell from grace when he was found to be a fraud, caught up in a juicing scandal in which he lied repeatedly about taking performance-enhancing drugs, leaving Armstrong disgraced.

Jean Genet / Miley Cyrus (88) In which your parents learn what "twerking" is. Former Disney teen star Miley Cyrus shook up her sweet image at the 2013 VMAs by getting low, thrusting her hips, and shaking her butt with unconcealed glee. Call it cultural appropriation or just bad taste, but there was no question that she owned it, just as Lysiane, the madam in Jean Genet's 1947 novel, *Querelle*, about power and sexuality in a French port town in the 1940s, unapologetically enjoys debauchery.

 Nikolai Gogol / *Terminator 2: Judgment Day* **(141)** Nikolai Gogol's *Dead Souls* is an 1842 satire set in a Russian village, but it beautifully describes the dismantling of gender roles in *Terminator 2*, the 1991 sequel to Arnold Schwarzenegger's star vehicle that celebrated masculinity and violence. *T2* features Linda Hamilton as a woman who is so determined to protect her son against assassins from the future that she nearly outshines her bulky costar. She becomes sleek and jacked and ready to fight— with Arnie's help, of course.

 Graham Greene / *Arrested Development* **(96)** Vodka for breakfast (and lunch and dinner and any time in between) is the coping method of choice for Lucille Bluth, matriarch of *Arrested Development*'s phenomenally dysfunctional family. As her husband tanks the family real-estate business, Lucille gets meaner, drunker, more inappropriate, and more hilarious with every martini. Graham Greene's 1948 novel *The Heart of the Matter* features an unhappy couple who make George and Lucille Bluth look like blissful newlyweds, with pink gin being their only relief from the drudgery of marriage.

 Graham Greene / Morrissey (114) The Smiths front man and beacon of perpetual sadness, Morrissey has made a decades-long career out of conveying misery that seems so singularly his that his adoring fans can't help but relate. The narrator of Graham Greene's 1951 novel, *The End of the Affair*, could have been a Morrissey fanboy, so consumed is he by romantic obsession and the mood swings that accompany it.

Thomas Hardy / *The Good Wife* (33) The politician caught with his pants down is an all-too-familiar trope both in real life and on TV, as is the dutiful wife who stands with stony eyes behind her husband and seems to try not to melt in anger and shame. But the CBS drama *The Good Wife* goes beyond cliché and explores just how Alicia Florrick becomes a true force of nature in her own right after her husband's scandal. Things don't turn out quite so well for the title character of Thomas Hardy's 1891 novel, *Tess of the D'Urbervilles*, who (spoiler alert) is destroyed by the sexual double standard and intolerance of the Victorian age. So let Alicia flourish in honor of all the wronged women who've come before.

 Nathaniel Hawthorne / *White Chicks* (80) *White Chicks* is a 2004 buddy comedy starring Marlon and Shawn Wayans as FBI agents who go deep, deep undercover. So deep, in fact, that they don whiteface to mix in with Vanessa Carlton–loving sorority girls. In his dark romanticism Nathaniel Hawthorne could probably never have imagined that his work would apply in such a scenario, but *White Chicks* is in fact a wonderful example of shared growth through unlikely friendships of which the omniscient narrator of *The Scarlet Letter* might have approved.

 Joseph Heller / Donald Trump (77) Perhaps no American tycoon better epitomizes the evils described in Joseph Heller's 1961 novel, *Catch-22*, about a young soldier trying to remain sane within a corrupt and morally bankrupt system, than Donald Trump. The real estate mogul, investor, wannabe politician, beauty pageant sponsor, President Obama truther, reality show host, and antivaccinationist contains the worst combination of arrogance and doublespeak that tend to comprise textbook catch-22s, in which absurdity rules and logic is cast aside.

Ernest Hemingway / *The Simpsons* (97) Homer Simpson's boss, Mr. Burns, is a caricature who embodies the personality traits of some of the most evil corporate executives of all time. Montgomery Burns's very best enabler is his faithful lapdog, Smithers, an executive assistant who has lived to please his boss decade after decade on *The Simpsons*. Smithers is the opposite of any kind of Hemingway hero: He's unctuous and lactose intolerant and prone to wearing cute bow ties, and always happy to subsume his own desires to please another man.

 Ernest Hemingway / *Twin Peaks* (54) Who killed Laura Palmer? David Lynch's 1990–1991 serial crime drama made viewers absolutely obsessed with figuring out the answer to this all-consuming question. When the lovely homecoming queen of Twin Peaks is found murdered and wrapped in plastic, her death turns out to be just the tip of the iceberg of the intense evil lurking in her "quiet" town. Innocence, as Hemingway wrote in his memoir, *A Moveable Feast*, about life as an expat in Paris in the 1920s, is more easily corruptible than any of us like to imagine.

 Aleksandar Hemon / *The Matrix* (106) In Aleksandar Hemon's 2008 novel, *The Lazarus Project*, a couple of Bosnian Americans in Chicago investigate a crime that took place a century earlier, intent on finding out the truth of what happened. In *The Matrix*, a 1999 sci-fi film, a rebellious hacker named Neo (Keanu Reeves) learns of a crime against humanity that has been taking place ever since the twenty-first century. In this dystopian future, machines rule the world and have set up a simulated reality for humans to inhabit. The truth is hard to swallow: When Neo takes a single red pill, he awakens to the terrible reality of his world, and he and his compatriots undertake a revolution against machines.

Amy Hempel / *American Idol* (20) While the audition episodes of reality TV contest *American Idol* are often bleaker than the worst night at a bad karaoke bar, they allowed the show's original judges—Simon, Paula, and Randy—to spout witticisms and criticisms and truisms while allowing home viewers sneak peeks of potential greatness to come. And each segment took just about three minutes—the same length of time it takes to devour the more bite-size short stories in Amy Hempel's vast, wonderful reserve. Three minutes is the perfect amount of time to come away with a distinct feeling about the quality of the work you've just heard or read, whether it's "that story was so profound" or "that singer should definitely keep his day job."

 Amy Hempel / Madonna (42) Madonna Louise Ciccone has made a decades-long career of superstardom out of juxtaposing religious imagery with overt sexuality. Her 1989 video for "Like a Prayer" is the apex of her stylish blasphemy, featuring a gorgeous gospel choir, a bunch of burning crosses, lots of gyration, and plenty of cleavage. As the narrator of Amy Hempel's novella "Tumble Home" observes, this elevation of sex over piety is nothing new—anyone who's read *Hamlet* in English class will know that.

 Patricia Highsmith / *Kill Bill: Volume 1* (82) In Quentin Tarantino's 2003 ultraviolent revenge film, Uma Thurman plays the Bride, a woman who has been wronged in perhaps the worst possible way, left for dead by a man who betrayed her. The embittered Bride becomes a killing machine, paying homage to martial arts movie icons like Bruce Lee. In master of suspense Patricia Highsmith's 1964 novel, *The Glass Cell*, a man who is wrongfully imprisoned understandably becomes angry and embittered over time, showing how injustice can make vengeance seekers out of the sweetest of people.

Alan Hollinghurst / *The Girl with the Dragon Tattoo* (139) David Fincher's 2011 adaptation of Swedish author Stieg Larsson's mega-best-selling thriller is almost unbearably unsettling in its dark subject matter and its relentless pacing. Alan Hollinghurst's 2004 novel, *The Line of Beauty*, is slow and sumptuous, and yet it shares with *The Girl with the Dragon Tattoo* an obsession with obsessions—a reverence for the kinds of deeply felt common interests that can bring people together in ways more powerful than love.

 Siri Hustvedt / *Gossip Girl* (126) In Siri Hustvedt's 2011 novel, *The Summer Without Men*, a woman retreats from both men and New York City after her marriage falls apart, moving to Minnesota to teach a poetry class for girls, most of whom are as cruel and as cliquey as adolescent girls tend to be. The hit CW series *Gossip Girl* makes an art out of girl-on-girl bitchery, with Blair Waldorf, the queen bee of the Upper East Side high school scene, as the bewitching ringleader. She and her minions sit on the steps at the Met, scheming and plotting, wearing super cute headbands and kilts that are the height of preppy fashion. As a bitter outsider observing these girls, the narrator of *Gossip Girl* skewers their lingo and their groupthink but simultaneously takes pleasure in their allure.

 Kazuo Ishiguro / *Dawson's Creek* (50) When Joey Potter climbs inside Dawson Leery's bedroom window on the WB teen drama *Dawson's Creek*, get ready for the dialogue to zing back and forth. Both innocent and wonderfully precocious—just like the protagonist in a film or two by Dawson's hero Steven Spielberg—Joey and Dawson explore the mysteries of adolescence, their friendly rapport barely hinting at the betrayals and heartbreaks that will come in future seasons. Kazuo Ishiguro's novel *Never Let Me Go* is also set in the 1990s, and creates a more sinister arc for three childhood friends who discover the very real dangers in growing up.

Henry James / *Beavis and Butt-Head* (105) "This sucks more than anything that has ever sucked before." Have there ever been realer, more honest culture critics than two teenage boys? MTV's Beavis and Butt-Head watched music videos and reacted with the sort of unfiltered disdain and enthusiasm that literary critic and novelist Henry James might have celebrated.

 Henry James / Gwyneth Paltrow (26) And now we come to *Star* magazine's Most Hated Celebrity of 2013, an actress who appears unlikely to know how much a gallon of milk costs—even organic nondairy milk! Gwyneth Paltrow, screen star and lifestyle guru (see her newsletter *Goop* for endorsements of a variety of luxury items), is what Henry James's inimitable heroine Isabel Archer could never be—in charge of her own brand.

 Leslie Jamison / *Mad Men* (102) Don Draper could be the sleek and shiny poster boy for the American Dream: he ditched a life of poverty to reinvent himself as a dashing, high-powered advertising exec. And yet. The hero (or is it antihero?) of AMC's *Mad Men* can't stop getting in his own way. He's not just the self-made man; he's also the destructive alcoholic, the selfish and petulant child, the man who thinks too often with his penis. In her 2014 collection of essays about empathy Leslie Jamison asks us to reconsider familiar tropes and where we traditionally place our sympathies. Draper is a deeply flawed man who might be most deserving of compassion when he's acting like a total jerk.

 Milan Kundera / *The X-Files* (128) *The X-Files*'s Scully and Mulder are FBI agents who work together to explain the inexplicable, and engage in the most charming repartee in the process. Their intense devotion to their jobs and their clearly smoldering chemistry make hunting down

UFOs seem so sexy. Milan Kundera's philosophical and romantic 1984 novel, *The Unbearable Lightness of Being*—about how every moment in life is singular, and therefore light—lays out relationship rules that are great in theory but rather impractical in practice.

 Rachel Kushner / One Direction (18) From Elvis and the Beatles to New Kids on the Block and Justin Bieber, teen idols have had the power to make young girls work themselves up into a frenzy. Harry Styles was the heartthrob of the moment in 2012 when One Direction appeared on the *Today* show and the sweet sound of thousands of shrieking adolescents filled Rockefeller Plaza. In Rachel Kushner's 2013 novel the youth screaming in the streets are participating in political unrest and revolution, not boy crushes. *The Flamethrowers* hints that perhaps the two phenomena are not as unrelated as we might think.

 Harper Lee / *Trading Places* (78) Harper Lee's groundbreaking 1960 novel, *To Kill a Mockingbird*, is a grade school classic because it tackles Big Issues about injustice and otherness and the importance of considering perspectives different from one's own. Meanwhile the 1983 comedy *Trading Places* takes the big life lessons of *Mockingbird* and presents them quite literally. Dan Aykroyd and Eddie Murphy star as a moneyed financier and a street hustler, respectively, who, for some ridiculous reason that only makes sense in the suspension-of-disbelief world of '80s movies, are forced to live each other's lives and discover all of the terrible assumptions based on race and class that Americans make about one another every day.

 Doris Lessing / *Married with Children* (157) Al and Peg Bundy seem to find a kind of bliss in their marital misery. While Doris Lessing's feminist first novel, *The Grass Is Singing*, ultimately proves the lack of value in this sort of relationship, the early 1990s FOX sitcom *Married*

With Children glorifies mutual unhappiness—the Bundys are most in their element when they're sitting on the couch, watching TV and bickering.

 Kelly Link / *Heathers* **(81)** "Dear diary, my teen-angst bullshit now has a body count." The 1988 comedy *Heathers* is a zillion times darker than your average teen movie, and for that reason we loved it. The movie depicts the utter despair of being a teenager and the ways that girls, in particular, can be monstrous to each other. Kelly Link has written a number of short stories that beautifully weave together the fantastical and the mundane, and *Pretty Monsters,* her first collection written specifically for young adult readers, captures the violence of childhood in ways in which *Heathers*'s Veronica Sawyer would surely approve.

 Clarice Lispector / *Breaking Bad* **(47)** The moral center of one of the greatest shows in the history of television is a high school dropout with awful fashion sense and a tendency to overuse the word "bitch." When Jesse Pinkman teams up with his former chemistry teacher to cook some of the best methamphetamine the New Mexico market has ever seen, both undergo transformations. AMC's *Breaking Bad* chronicles Mr. White's evolution from simple high school teacher to drug kingpin, but it also follows the growth of his partner, Jesse Pinkman, who discovers his own decency and morality even as Walt leads them to darker and darker places. Clarice Lispector's posthumously published 1977 novel, *The Hour of the Star*, is set in the slums of Rio de Janeiro, a dog-eat-dog world where questioning one's humanity can seem like the only sane thing to do.

 Hilary Mantel / *Star Wars* **(74)** It turns out that the sixteenth-century England ruled by King Henry VIII and the Galactic Empire ruled by Darth Vader long, long ago have quite a bit in common. Hilary

Mantel's historical novels offer a multidimensional portrait of Thomas Cromwell's rise to power in the court of King Henry VIII, but Cromwell's theory that power requires a certain air of mystery seems like a direct shout-out to *Star Wars*'s heavy-breathing masked villain.

W. Somerset Maugham / *Cheers* (158) Sam and Diane of the 1980s sitcom *Cheers* are the textbook example of the love-hate relationship. Just as the narrator of Somerset Maugham's 1915 masterpiece, *Of Human Bondage*, is tormented by his all-consuming love for a woman who's rather mean to him, bar employees Sam and Diane give off a palpable air of lust in even their most heated arguments.

W. Somerset Maugham / Michael Jordan (10) If a Michael Jordan slam dunk isn't art, what is? See the Chicago Bulls superstar soar through the air as the NBA's 1988 Slam Dunk Contest winner. Basketball was probably not what British author Somerset Maugham had in mind when he described his idea of beauty in his 1925 novel, *The Painted Veil*, but it's breathtaking all the same.

Colum McCann / *Friday Night Lights* (12) The relationship between Eric and Tami Taylor, a.k.a. Coach and Mrs. Coach, might just be the truest and sweetest depiction of a marriage ever shown on television. The *Friday Night Lights* couple is the heart of the drama about high school football in a small Texas town. Colum McCann's 2009 ode to New York, *Let the Great World Spin*, weaves together the stories of a swath of characters from all walks of city life, including a wealthy, unhappy couple living on the Upper East Side. There may not be two more distinctly unique settings in America than New York City and Dillon, Texas, but the show and the novel both so aptly capture how the beauty of long-term relationships can be universal.

Cormac McCarthy / *Buffy the Vampire Slayer* (71) Cormac McCarthy's postapocalyptic 2006 novel, *The Road*, may just be the bleakest Oprah's Book Club pick of all time, all darkness and death and misery. Buffy Summers, the California Valley girl and heroine of Joss Whedon's groundbreaking TV series *Buffy the Vampire Slayer*, is all sunshine and light until she encounters a vampire or any other monster, and then she becomes an efficient exterminator. The contrast between Buffy's cuteness and her deadly force is played for humor, but the teen action series has surprisingly weighty philosophical themes that would fit right into a McCarthy novel. After all, the burden of living right near a Hellmouth and constantly having to fight evil can take its toll on even the most well-adjusted heroine.

Elizabeth McCracken / *The OC* (122) Elizabeth McCracken's 1996 novel, *The Giant's House*, about the romantic life of a small-town librarian delineates the obsessive tendencies that make bibliophiles feel alive. There is no better embodiment of passionate compulsion than *The OC*'s Seth Cohen, the bookworm/music lover/comic book fan/cinephile who makes being a total nerd seem so, so cool.

Carson McCullers / *The Office* (68) Dwight Schrute and Angela Kinsey do not comprise the primary workplace romance on NBC's hit sitcom *The Office* (romcom-ready Jim and Pam have that honor). But this couple of weirdos would have fit in well among the band of misfits who populate Carson McCullers's most celebrated novel about life and loneliness in a small town, *The Heart Is a Lonely Hunter*. Angela and Dwight have their own undeniable chemistry, one that is celebrated in the 2013 series finale episode about their wedding day.

Ian McEwan / Mark Zuckerberg (113) Who knew that an elderly woman in the late 1990s reflecting back on her life could so well predict a twenty-first-century phenomenon? Ian McEwan's 2001 novel, *Atonement*, about love and war and regret mostly takes place in World War II–era England, but in the present day his narrator comments on the blurring lines between social classes. Her remark predicts the rise of the slovenly billionaires, tech entrepreneurs like Mark Zuckerberg, who, just a few short years later, would come to cofound Facebook. Today we know we must never judge a social media guru's bank account by the quality of his flip-flops.

Herman Melville / *Homeland* (35) Showtime's dramatic series *Homeland* stars Claire Danes as Carrie Mathison, a bipolar CIA agent with a feverish work ethic and an Internet GIF-worthy cry face. The show's first season, in 2011, introduces Carrie to her white whale: Nicholas Brody, a former marine and prisoner of war who has recently been returned home to America and who may or may not have been brainwashed by the enemy into becoming an al-Qaeda operative. Herman Melville's tragic Captain Ahab is one of literature's most enduring symbols for the way obsession can destroy a man, but Carrie's fixation with Brody is trickier to categorize: Is her illness manifesting itself in a rainbow of manic colors on her living room wall, or is there a logical, heroic method to her madness?

Lorrie Moore / *Dirty Dancing* (8) In the 1980s *Dirty Dancing* was the go-to videotape for sheltered suburban girls who yearned to leap into womanhood with the help of a streetwise older man who had a great butt and a killer soundtrack. No living author is better than Lorrie Moore at revealing the agonies and delights of losing one's innocence, the creeping uncertainty that separates girlish wishes from reality.

Lorrie Moore / *Waiting to Exhale* (111) *Waiting to Exhale*, the 1995 film adaptation of Terry McMillan's novel of the same name, celebrates the real talk, sympathy, and support that four girlfriends offer to each other. Led by Bernadine and Savannah (played by Angela Bassett and Whitney Houston), the four women come together to drink wine, bitch, sympathize, laugh with and empower one another, no prepackaged clichés required. Lorrie Moore's 1997 short story "People Like That Are the Only People Here" takes place in a children's oncology ward and is brutally sad, but it also contains an appreciation for friends who can cut through the bullshit and offer a small bit of comfort in times of tragedy.

 Toni Morrison / *Felicity* (147) Felicity Porter and her head full of curls arrive at the fictional University of New York in 1998, ostensibly to follow her high school crush to college, but more to experience life in a new city and make it her own. The J. J. Abrams series *Felicity* follows Ms. Porter and her group of friends as they navigate their studies and their relationships and the streets of Greenwich Village to find out who they are. Felicity's downtown college experience varies greatly from Toni Morrison's depiction of African Americans in Harlem in the Jazz Age of the 1920s, *Jazz*, but what unites these two narratives is the sense of possibility that lingers on every corner of New York City.

 Alice Munro / *Parks and Recreation* (32) Alice Munro's story "Silence" includes a description of a woman who may or may not be the leader of a cult—certainly not a pleasant connotation. However, the quote also applies to one of TV's most adored characters: Leslie Knope, who enjoys team-building exercises and office supplies just as much as she loves waffles and Ben Wyatt's cute butt. The NBC sitcom *Parks & Recreation*, led by Amy Poehler, pulls off an amazing feat: it makes a blindingly optimistic, rules-adoring bureaucrat absolutely lovable.

Alice Munro / *Veronica Mars* (117) The Canadian queen of short stories, Alice Munro, is the perfect author to pair with teen detective and overall feminist role model Veronica Mars. Munro's stories about the lives of complicated women and girls tend to move about in time, as does Veronica's: the first season of the UPN TV series features flashbacks that reveal Veronica's charmed life before her best friend was murdered, while current-day Veronica is an outcast who begins to question authority and think critically about her fellow residents in the economically stratified town of Neptune, California. As played by Kristen Bell, Veronica is clever and tough, armed with enough smarts and sarcasm to solve many crimes and foil many villains, even as a palpable anger lingers just below her surface.

 Haruki Murakami / *Groundhog Day* (127) Novelist Haruki Murakami writes some of the most imaginative fiction of the current day, but in his foray into nonfiction—a 2008 memoir about marathon running—he shifts more to the methodical and mundane. Meanwhile, the 1993 comedy *Groundhog Day* proves that the effort of living through one day can sometimes literally become a marathon event. Bill Murray plays a cynical weatherman who must endure endless same-days of reporting on Punxsutawney Phil and being awoken to "I Got You Babe," until he finally makes a proper transformation.

 Haruki Murakami / Michael Jackson (17) It takes extraordinary talent to make a seemingly simple dance move look like nothing less than a work of art. In his 1992 novel, *South of the Border, West of the Sun*, Haruki Murakami captures the motivation of so many of the denizens of Japanese jazz clubs, their willingness to sit through myriad mediocre sets in the hopes of catching that one special performance that might prove transcendent. Michael Jackson's moonwalk was his own superhuman feat, a trademark step that was uniquely his own, emblematic of the magic that made MJ the king of pop.

Iris Murdoch / *True Detective* **(44)** The unreliable narrator is the subject of Iris Murdoch's 1978 novel, *The Sea, the Sea*, about a self-satisfied playwright who reveals a startlingly deluded view of his world as he holes up in his seaside home to write his memoir. Unreliable narrators were also the centerpiece of HBO's 2014 series that gave affable pothead bros Matthew McConaughey and Woody Harrelson, playing troubled cops who are hot on the trail of a serial killer, a chance to show their more philosophical sides.

 Vladimir Nabokov / *Lady Gaga* **(38)** It takes a lot of work for a pop star to constantly shock and awe at every appearance, on every red carpet and runway and photo shoot. At the 2010 VMAs Lady Gaga wore her legendary meat dress, an ensemble made out of raw beef. Vladimir Nabokov—himself a first-rate provocateur—often wrote about the phenomenon of doubling, encountering duplicates of main characters and mirror images of related events. The role that Gaga assumes as button pusher is perhaps not so rare (sorry!) among those who must vie for the spotlight and can therefore seem duplicative, if not interchangeable.

 Joyce Carol Oates / *Basic Instinct* **(129)** Perhaps one of the most high-concept novels that prolific author Joyce Carol Oates has ever written is her 2000 imagining of the inner life of Marilyn Monroe. *Blonde* contemplates the glamorization of female madness, the irony that Marilyn could be so universally adored and yet so unbalanced inside. Joe Eszterhas's skeevy 1992 erotic thriller certainly glamorizes madness as Sharon Stone's blond bombshell Catherine Tramell famously uncrosses her legs while discussing her skills with an ice pick. The stuff of fantasies, whether or not she's a sociopathic killer.

Joyce Carol Oates / *Fargo* **(52)** Marge Gunderson is a pregnant police officer who has a loving marriage, a zest for life, a fantastic accent, and a home in Minnesota where it seems like the dark days of winter could descend over the frozen, flat landscape forever. Throughout *Fargo*, the Coen brothers' 1996 film about the perpetrators of a series of botched crimes, Marge is unflaggingly optimistic even when she's called out of her cozy bed to investigate incompetent felons. Joyce Carol Oates's 2012 novel, *Mudwoman*, about a female president of a prestigious college whose life intersects with an abused and abandoned child touches on the accomplishment of remaining happy in the darkest of places.

 Flannery O'Connor / *The Wonder Years* **(100)** The 1980s sitcom *The Wonder Years* was a nostalgic paradise for baby boomers. Narrated from the point of view of a grown man (Daniel Stern) reminiscing about his childhood in a generic American suburb in the late '60s and early '70s, *The Wonder Years* was a loving ode to the coming-of-age of a young boy and of a nation in general. According to Flannery O'Connor's essays and articles published posthumously, her childhood in Savannah, Georgia, seemed ordinary enough, certainly not an indicator of the violence that would later appear in her gothic fiction. The simple act of growing up itself is brutal enough, it seems, to acquire a level of worldliness.

 Jenny Offill / *Glee* **(95)** McKinley High's resident power couple Blaine and Kurt (Darren Criss and Chris Colfer) fell in and out and in and out of love through several showstoppers on Glee, FOX's hit a cappella series. *Dept. of Speculation*, Jenny Offill's novel of a marriage, one of the simplest, truest depictions of love and heartbreak in literature, is at its best when it celebrates the profundity of even the cheesiest pop song.

Michael Ondaatje / *Downton Abbey* (24) Michael Ondaatje's 2011 novel, *The Cat's Table*, takes place on a ship traveling from Ceylon (now Sri Lanka) to England, as Michael, an eleven-year-old boy, takes in all of the spectacles of the voyage even from his vantage point at the least-esteemed table on the boat. The ship encompasses the very different lifestyles of all the people in its uppermost berths and lower decks. On *Downton Abbey*, the British series broadcast in America on PBS about all of the people living under the same roof of an English manor about a century ago, it's clear that great power shifts are in place for both the family who lives upstairs and the staff who dine and live in the floors below.

 Ann Patchett / *Clueless* (30) In *Truth & Beauty* Ann Patchett celebrates her intimate friendship with *Autobiography of a Face* author Lucy Grealy, and the ways their bond could be more intense than any romantic relationship. The idea that close friends can create their own special lingo based on mutual understanding is a central reason why Amy Heckerling's 1995 comedy, *Clueless*, features so many memorable moments and quotable lines. Cher Horowitz's best friend, Dionne Davenport, supports her in all endeavors, whether it's shopping, makeovers, prepping for a hot date, learning to drive, or remaining "hymenally challenged" because Cher is saving herself for Luke Perry.

 Hannah Pittard / *Freaks and Geeks* (93) Hannah Pittard's 2012 debut novel is narrated in the first person plural—"we"—which is the voice of a group of suburban boys who are left reeling by the disappearance of a classmate. On a happier note, Judd Apatow and Paul Feig's love letter to early 1980s high school awkwardness ran on NBC for one glorious season. Featuring future buddy comedy superstars James Franco and Seth Rogen, *Freaks and Geeks* flourished on DVDs and streaming services and remains a cult classic. For all that the *Freaks and Geeks* characters often feel like outsiders, their stories are told in the best sense of the word "we"—cohesive groups of friends within the chaos of high school.

 Sylvia Plath / *The Bachelor* (36) Sylvia Plath certainly wasn't the first writer to view dating as sport, but the 2000 publication of her unabridged journals, which she wrote in the 1950s, was particularly perfect timing. Two years after the publication of her journals, *The Bachelor* debuted on ABC and introduced the concept that fame and marriage can be the ultimates in game show prizes. Viewers watch an eligible gentleman go through the weeks-long process of whittling down twenty-five hopefuls to find his one true love, all while cameras film the entire courtship. Inevitably, the contestants who are not offered roses at the ceremony in which the bachelor chooses the contestants who will move on to the next episode leave in tears. Whether they're tears of genuine Sylvia Plath–level heartbreak and disillusionment or simple disappointment in losing a game, it's often hard to tell.

 Francine Prose / *Lost* (149) The only setting more terrifying than the mysterious island onto which Oceanic Flight 815 crash-lands on ABC's hit series *Lost* is the former death camp where a Kafka conference is being held in Francine Prose's 1997 novella "Guided Tours of Hell." Yikes! A Kafka symposium attendee takes a moment away from nursing his academic jealousies to contemplate the life decisions of a Holocaust survivor, and realizes that it's difficult to judge anyone who's lived through such horror.

 Marcel Proust / *The Shawshank Redemption* (138) The first volume of Marcel Proust's *Remembrance of Things Past* is a collection of memories of the narrator's boyhood, memories so involuntary that the mere taste of a madeleine cake can bring a flood of forgotten recollections rushing back. The 1994 film adaptation of Stephen King's novella takes place at

Shawshank State Prison, and stars Morgan Freeman and Tim Robbins as inmates whose present lives are so desolate that all they have is their memories and the power to hope that the future will bring solace.

 Philip Roth / Bill Clinton and Monica Lewinsky (121) The Bill Clinton–Monica Lewinsky affair was nearly cinematic in its absurdity, the leader of the free world almost ruined by phenomenally bad decision-making, symbolized by a stain on an intern's little blue Gap dress. Thank you, then, to Philip Roth, for being one of the best living writers of our time, and also for being a great source of material when searching for quotes about the motives of lecherous older men. Meanwhile, Lewinsky, after years of shame and public mockery, has risen from the ashes of the scandal to be an inspiring and quotable speaker in her own right.

 Norman Rush / *Roseanne* (92) The narrator of Norman Rush's 1991 novel, *Mating*, is a wayward postgrad student who is both tremendously intelligent and delightfully foolish. She gets a lot of things wrong in her anthropological research, but she's spot-on in her insight that intimate comedy is necessary for a happy relationship. Dan and Roseanne Conner of the ABC sitcom *Roseanne* would make a great case study for *Mating*'s narrator: even in the midst of the everyday struggles of a blue-collar family trying to stay afloat, they manage to be delighted by each other.

 Salman Rushdie / *Ghostbusters* (144) New York City was never so beautiful and slimy as when a bunch of nerds with backpacks full of protons faced off with a giant-size Stay Puft Marshmallow Man to rid the city of paranormal activities in the 1984 movie comedy *Ghostbusters*. Salman Rushdie's *Fury* is also set in New York—one of the British Indian author's only novels to take place in the United States—and yet Rushdie aptly distills the magnificent contradictions of American city life.

Salman Rushdie / *Six Feet Under* (70) Each episode of the HBO dramedy *Six Feet Under* opens with a death, most notably the death of the patriarch of the Fisher family in the premier episode. The subsequent episodes follow Nathaniel Fisher Sr.'s surviving relatives as they go about trying to keep the family business afloat—a funeral home where they're surrounded by ghosts, metaphorical and otherwise. The ghosts in Salman Rushdie's novel *The Satanic Verses*, whose criticism of Islam enraged Ayatollah Khomeini of Iran so greatly that he issued a fatwa calling for the execution of the author, are mostly found in the dream sequences of a schizophrenic Bollywood star haunted by alienation and his ever-worsening disease.

Richard Russo / *Thelma & Louise* (116) "I don't ever remember feeling this awake," says Thelma, one of the titular heroines of the 1991 feminist manifesto of a film in which two friends flee their unsatisfying lives and set off on a disaster-filled yet empowering road trip. In 2001 Richard Russo won the Pulitzer Prize for Fiction for *Empire Falls*, a novel about Miles, the manager of a small-town diner, and his family. On a smaller scale, Miles's teenage daughter has a *Thelma & Louise*–style awakening when she gathers the perspective to see through an ex-boyfriend's bullshit and realize how freeing the act of not giving a damn can be.

J. D. Salinger / *The Osbournes* (119) According to the MTV reality show of the early aughts, Ozzy Osbourne, the heavy metal star who once bit the head off a bat onstage, is just a zany family man with a doting wife, wacky kids, and a menagerie of cute dogs. In some ways, the Osbournes do very much resemble the members of the Glass family of whom J. D. Salinger would so often write. The pleasure of watching the show is tied to the voyeuristic delight of witnessing the tics and rituals and eccentricities that are particular to the Osbourne family.

Jean-Paul Sartre / *Seinfeld* (60) When we consider the great existential philosophers of the twentieth century, please remember to include Jerry Seinfeld on the list, right after Albert Camus and Jean-Paul Sartre. Seinfeld, along with Larry David, created a "show about nothing" that is as existentialist as any NBC sitcom has been before or since. *Seinfeld* focuses on the mundane little dramas of everyday life and inflates them to major plot points—the show makes getting lost in a parking garage or waiting to be seated at a Chinese restaurant seem like epic adventures.

 George Saunders / *The Daily Show* (55) George Saunders is a short story writer and humorist whose 2007 collection, *The Braindead Megaphone*, contains an essay called "Mr. Vonnegut in Sumatra," in which he describes how his reading of Kurt Vonnegut affected his understanding of comedy. Saunders admires the way Vonnegut uses irony and sincerity simultaneously, a feat Jon Stewart pulled off nightly until his retirement from *The Daily Show*, the Comedy Central show that turned fake news into an incredibly popular genre of comedy that favors both silliness and blunt honesty.

 Carol Shields / Wedding of William and Kate (4) The 2011 nuptials of Prince William and Kate Middleton were as elegant as a royal wedding could be—that is, until an adorably pissed-off three-year-old, William's goddaughter, offered another perspective on the otherwise fairy-tale-like day. Canadian author Carol Shields wrote in her 1993 novel, *The Stone Diaries*, about how rites of passage depend so much on the interpretations of others, and it's fun to imagine antiroyalists making that little girl their poster child.

Betty Smith / Justin Timberlake and Britney Spears (150) In the early aughts Britney Spears and Justin Timberlake were so in sync that even the music megastars' spectacularly tacky denim ensembles complemented each other perfectly. Francie Nolan, the teenage heroine of Betty Smith's 1943 novel, *A Tree Grows in Brooklyn*, also comes to learn that there's nothing quite as heady as the thrill of first love. But Francie eventually moves on from heartbreak, as did Brit and Justin—and we have their nasty breakup to thank for great songs like "Cry Me a River."

 Patti Smith / *Lost in Translation* (49) In her 2010 memoir, *Just Kids*, singer and poet Patti Smith reflects on her young and poor days in New York City with her partner in crime, photographer Robert Mapplethorpe. Smith's quote about the companionship of their youth equally applies to Sofia Coppola's 2003 film, *Lost In Translation*, in which two lonely souls played by Scarlett Johansson and Bill Murray meet in Tokyo and form an unlikely bond. Sometimes feeling comfortable in a scary new city requires dependence on an equally out-of-sorts companion with whom to make great art, or just to sing karaoke.

 Zadie Smith / *Sex and the City* (67) The HBO series *Sex and the City* stars Sarah Jessica Parker as Carrie Bradshaw, a relationship columnist who documents the ups and downs of her dating life in New York City, and the perpetual quest for designer shoes. The characters in Zadie Smith's 2000 debut novel, *White Teeth*, are just as witty as Carrie and her crew, but their concerns about race and immigrant life in London are a wonderful reminder that there's a wide world out there that's so much more than couture and cosmos and dating disasters.

Zadie Smith / *30 Rock* (112) In Zadie Smith's 2005 novel, *On Beauty*, Zora Belsey dresses the part as she hopes to reinvent herself at the start of her sophomore year of college. *30 Rock*'s Liz Lemon is a high-powered TV exec with genius creative vision who also happens to be a goober—her idea of a fun night involves eating cheese on her couch while wearing a Snuggie. Certainly she doesn't ever intend to be a traditional bride, so when it's time to say her "I dos" with Criss Chros, Lemon takes a page from Zora Belsey, forgoing a pouffy dress and veil in favor of any *Star Wars* fan's most loving approximation of a wedding gown—a lovely white Princess Leia sheath and two perfect side buns.

 Rebecca Solnit / *Young Adult* (155) You can't go home again, as Mavis Gary finds in the 2011 comedy *Young Adult*. As Mavis, Charlize Theron plays the prom queen turned sour—a beautiful woman with big sunglasses and Ugg boots and an adorable purse dog who is distinctly lonely, sad, and unfulfilled. Rebecca Solnit's 2005 essay collection, *A Field Guide to Getting Lost*, focuses on places—how where we are makes us who we are, and how time is fleeting but places remain. Sadly for Mavis, when she returns to her childhood home and the site of her former glory days, it becomes apparent that the people who populate her memories are not as unchangeable as they are in her mind.

 Susan Sontag / Kanye West (91) Susan Sontag was one of the sharpest observers of our culture—so much so that she understood the particular power of her own image. Sontag was constantly aware of the effect she had on others, as is Kanye West, a hip-hop star whose command of the spectacle of himself has transformed outrageous narcissism into art.

Susan Sontag / *24* (148) In her final book published before her death in 2004, essayist and cultural critic Susan Sontag grappled with the moral consequences of witnessing atrocities—particularly in photographic form. Meanwhile, for most of the first decade of the twenty-first century, TV viewers could tune in weekly to *24* and watch fictional depictions of torture in their living rooms in real time. When even dashing TV heroes like Kiefer Sutherland's Jack Bauer use and normalize horrific interrogation techniques that Sontag strongly spoke out against before her death, the real-life revelations of the CIA's 2014 torture report felt nearly inevitable.

 Edward St. Aubyn / *Twilight* (131) The teen fantasy saga based on Stephenie Meyer's best-selling book series features the beautiful vampire Edward Cullen, whose domineering ways and patronizing overprotection of his human ladyfriend, Bella, provided inspiration for the *Fifty Shades of Grey* trilogy. Edward St. Aubyn's Patrick Melrose is also an arrogant and privileged man born of an elite but tragic bloodline, but he's rather less worthy of fan fiction. Instead of a lust for blood, the twenty-two-year-old addict craves drugs the most, with the vague idea of sex coming in a distant second.

 Wallace Stegner / *Working Girl* (89) With determination nearly as high as her best friend's teased bangs, secretary Tess McGill puts on power suits and running shoes and hops on the Staten Island Ferry to Manhattan, all to the tune of Carly Simon's "Let the River Run." Throughout it all her unexpectedly wise friend Cyn (Joan Cusack) is there to offer her own tips on how to succeed in business as Tess plots to become an executive with her own office. Wallace Stegner's novel *Crossing to Safety* about a circle of friends with writerly ambition celebrates the support systems that allow determination such as Tess's to flourish.

John Steinbeck / *Revenge of the Nerds* **(137)** John Steinbeck's 1939 masterpiece depicts the tribulations of disenfranchised tenant farmers during the Great Depression and the Dust Bowl. Just as *The Grapes of Wrath*'s Joad family searches for common decency and a little dignity, so do the brothers of Lambda Lambda Lambda. Yes, this comparison of wannabe frat boys being bullied by a bunch of jocks in a 1984 comedy to a family that has come to symbolize the American struggle is crass, but the sentiment is universal: the oppressed must grow stronger when faced with terrible adversity.

 John Steinbeck / *The Wolf of Wall Street* **(90)** John Steinbeck wrote from the point of view of America's underclass, the laborers and farmhands whose voices are so often marginalized by the wealthier and more fortunate. The story of Jordan Belfort is such a gross derangement of capitalism and of rich megalomaniacs triumphing over the middle and lower classes that even John Steinbeck couldn't have imagined it. The subject of the 2014 film *The Wolf of Wall Street* starring Leonardo DiCaprio, Belfort is a stockbroker who scammed millions of dollars from hundreds of clients. His taste for the trappings of success (drugs and women and sports cars) and power above all else is abhorrent, but it's also fascinating. Audiences were titillated by the very things we are supposed to despise, and Belfort became some kind of twisted folk hero all over again.

 Donna Tartt / *Black Swan* **(66)** Donna Tartt's debut novel, *The Secret History*, chronicles the unraveling of a tight-knit group of pretentious students who study the classics at a liberal arts college. Their intellectual justifications for their shockingly sinister undertakings seem downright ridiculous, but there may be some truth to the claim that beauty is to be feared. Darren Aronofsky's psychological thriller *Black Swan* stars Natalie

Portman as an aspiring ballerina on the edge of a nervous breakdown, flirting with madness in the most beautiful and terrifying way.

 Donna Tartt / *Scandal* (64) *Scandal*'s Olivia Pope is the sleek Washington, DC, fixer who seemingly can solve everyone's problems but her own: her wardrobe is impeccable, but her heart is unkempt. That she loves a handsome politician who runs the nation as the president on a Shonda Rhimes drama should (very passionately and recklessly) only makes the show more addictive. Donna Tartt's epic 2014 Pulitzer Prize–winning novel, *The Goldfinch*, chronicles the equally self-destructive Theo Decker as he follows his own heart's desire: drugs and a missing Dutch masterpiece.

 Colm Tóibín / *The Royal Tenenbaums* (58) Colm Tóibín's 2006 short story collection, *Mothers and Sons*, explores a wide variety of complex family dynamics, but perhaps no fictional family is quite as blissfully dysfunctional as Wes Anderson's Tenenbaums. Chas, Margot, and Richie are three former prodigies whose adult lives are not nearly as fulfilling as their childhoods were. When their father summons them back to their childhood home, we see how weird and gorgeous they are in their shared misery, particularly Richie Tenenbaum (Luke Wilson) and his adoptive sister, Margot (Gwyneth Paltrow), whose tortured love for each other provides poignant scenes of intimacy and also many laughs.

 Leo Tolstoy / *Orange Is the New Black* (43) Of course the Netflix original series *Orange Is the New Black* brings Tolstoy to mind— the details of life in a women's prison in upper New York State call out for comparisons to Russian literature. *OITNB* is the story of Piper Chapman, an upper-middle-class white woman who must give up the privileged existence she took for granted when she's sentenced to prison for a crime she committed years ago. Jail is horrifying to Piper, as it is to all of its inmates, and perhaps she finds a bit of grace in being forced to accept and identify with women whose life experiences are so very different from her own.

 Kurt Vonnegut / *Beverly Hills, 90210* (1) *Slaughterhouse-Five* is a modern masterpiece that features alien planets and traumatized war vets and time travel, so of course it pairs perfectly with a nighttime drama about a bunch of kids from LA's poshest zip code. Really! *Beverly Hills, 90210* was the aspirational soap opera of the 1990s, and the Walsh home was the perfect little safe place where everything was OK. The show was the kind of beautiful dream that would have comforted Vonnegut's Billy Pilgrim in times of distress—Casa Walsh would the perfect retreat. Plus, Vonnegut is definitely an author whose oeuvre brooding heartthrob Dylan McKay probably would've dug.

 Kurt Vonnegut / *Jersey Shore* (76) Amid all the fist pumping and gym-tan-laundrying that happened during MTV's breakout 2009 reality show *Jersey Shore*, a pint-size binge drinker with a filthy mouth became a sensation. Snooki Polizzi was the show's breakout star, in part because she was naturally hilarious in front of the camera. Her style and attitude and her catchphrases ("Party's here!") made her a perfect embodiment of the kind of farting around of which Vonnegut himself was a proponent.

 David Foster Wallace / *America's Next Top Model* (154) Observe the smoldering intensity of Tyra Banks as she schools legions of hopefuls on walking a runway in six-inch platform heels without wobbling, or the utter importance of mastering the art of the "smize" (smiling with one's eyes). It's enough to make a great subject for a David Foster Wallace essay about the absurdity of our popular culture and the frivolities that obsess us. The footnotes alone would be fierce.

Evelyn Waugh / *Mean Girls* (135) In both *Brideshead Revisited* and *Mean Girls*, a young and pliable outsider is granted access to another world, glimpsing a new way of life in which it's terribly difficult to avoid being swept up. Evelyn Waugh's 1945 novel concerns a middle-class college student who, when invited on a holiday at his friend's family's grand estate—they actually own a castle—finds his life becomes inextricably linked with theirs. The 2004 comedy *Mean Girls* stars Lindsay Lohan as Cady Heron, a girl raised in Africa by zoologists who learns that the rules of the jungle apply very nicely in the suburbs. Cady infiltrates the popular crowd at high school in order to study the girls like a scientist, only to be seduced by the advantages of sitting at the cool table.

 Edith Wharton / *Brokeback Mountain* (59) A disgraced countess and an aristocratic lawyer in New York City in the 1870s. A ranch hand and a rodeo cowboy in the Wyoming mountains in the 1960s. The characters in Edith Wharton's *The Age of Innocence* and Ang Lee's film adaptation of Annie Proulx's 1997 short story *Brokeback Mountain* live in completely different worlds, but they are all victims of unforgiving American mores. Both tales explore the agonies of forbidden relationships and excoriate our society's lack of tolerance in the face of love.

 Edith Wharton / Tina Fey and Amy Poehler (85) In her 1934 autobiography, *A Backward Glance*, Edith Wharton wrote much about her bond with Henry James and the power of sharing a similar point of view with a good friend. From cohosting *Saturday Night Live*'s "Weekend Update" to cohosting the Golden Globe Awards together, the power duo of Tina Fey and Amy Poehler are always in glorious harmony. The besties have countless projects as individuals, but when they come together, it always feels extra special—the comedy equivalent of literary legends seeing eye to eye.

Colson Whitehead / Beyoncé (72) In one flawless performance at the 2014 MTV Video Music Awards, Beyoncé single-handedly reclaimed a powerful word that had gotten a bad rap in pop culture. Queen Bey reminded the world that feminism comes in many forms, and that being politically conscious and sexy as hell are not mutually exclusive. If we don't necessarily expect all of our pop singers to be heroes, Colson Whitehead's 2011 zombie novel shows how agency and opportunity make superstars in times of distress: in *Zone One* he shares a few examples, including a former porn star turned political hotshot, mostly because she has a very particular skill—kicking the ass of the undead.

 Oscar Wilde / *Mrs. Doubtfire* (120) Oscar Wilde's Dorian Gray is a beautiful young man who wishes to hold on to his youth eternally, even as his portrait ages and withers with time. The title character in *Mrs. Doubtfire* is perfectly happy to do the opposite—the 1993 comedy stars Robin Williams as a dad who dons glasses, a gray wig, and a fat suit to go undercover as an elderly British nanny in order to spend more time with his kids after separating from his wife.

 Oscar Wilde / *Pulp Fiction* (75) Quentin Tarantino is a master of making films that feature beautifully stylized violence, none more so than his 1994 blockbuster, *Pulp Fiction*. Samuel L. Jackson costars as killer-for-hire Jules Winnfield, an immaculately dressed fast-food hamburger connoisseur who is known to quote dramatic chunks of the Bible (Ezekiel 25:17) when carrying out a hit. Much like the title character of Oscar Wilde's 1891 novel, *The Picture of Dorian Gray*, Jules turns even the basest forms of evil into an art form, and he looks great doing it.

Jeanette Winterson / *Eternal Sunshine of the Spotless Mind* **(107)** Jeanette Winterson is a go-to writer for readers tormented by lost love—her novels detail the ways that doubt and grief and jealousy can creep in when relationships end badly. In Michel Gondry and Charlie Kaufman's fantastical 2004 film, *Eternal Sunshine of the Spotless Mind*, Jim Carrey and Kate Winslet play Joel and Clementine, a broken-up couple so desperate to forget they ever met that they undergo a procedure to delete memories of each other from their brains. But even as the erasure begins to take place, somewhere in Joel's unconscious their romance lives on as vividly and brightly as the variety of colors of Clementine's hair.

 Jeanette Winterson / *The Great Muppet Caper* **(27)** In the early 1980s there was perhaps no better role model for impressionable young girls than Miss Piggy. The most unapologetically aggressive Muppet, she was more than happy to karate chop anyone or anything that got in her way, both in her acting career and in her love for a sweet little green frog. The gender of the unnamed narrator of Jeanette Winterson's 1993 novel, *Written on the Body*, about a tumultuous love affair, remains a mystery throughout the book, but glamour-puss diva Piggy is a lovely embodiment of the intense, all-consuming passion that Winterson writes of so lyrically.

 P. G. Wodehouse / *Fight Club* **(6)** P. G. Wodehouse and Chuck Palahniuk have nearly polar opposite sensibilities. Wodehouse is all charm and subtle wit, while Palahniuk is probably the kind of guy who uses ALL CAPS in all his e-mails—his anger is apparent in nearly every line of his work. However, Wodehouse has good insight into the dangers of giving in to one's subconscious, as does David Fincher's highly visceral 1999 adaptation of Palahniuk's novel that stars Brad Pitt and Edward Norton as members of that club you're not supposed to talk about.

P. G. Wodehouse / *Harry Potter and the Chamber of Secrets* (15) The screen adaptation of the second installment of J. K. Rowling's series about the education and development of adolescent wizards features many wise characters, but none so determined as Hermione Granger, the most put-together twelve-year-old witch to ever cast a spell. She is a shining example of the kind of precocious young girls that P. G. Wodehouse blithely references in *Uneasy Money*, his one-off 1916 novel about love, golf, and the fundamental differences between men and women.

 Tobias Wolff / *The Hunger Games* (83) "I volunteer as tribute!" With four powerful little words, Katniss Everdeen starts a revolution in a film based on the mega-best-selling trilogy by Suzanne Collins set in a dystopian society in which children are forced to compete to the death in a televised reality show. As Tobias Wolff recounts in his 1989 memoir of growing up in a violent household, *This Boy's Life*, the power shift from oppressor to oppressee can happen rapidly when the weak make clear that they are willing to fight for freedom and respect.

 Meg Wolitzer / *Romy and Michele's High School Reunion* (94) Meg Wolitzer's 2013 novel, *The Interestings*, chronicles the lifelong friendships of a group of kids who meet at a summer camp for the arts in 1974. Some go on to astounding success, and some never quite achieve the heights that their creativity and ambition once promised. In the 1997 comedy *Romy and Michele's High School Reunion*, the title characters aren't exactly ambitious, but you can't say that they're not creative (look at their wardrobes!), and their imaginations are both expansive and severely limited. See, for example, their plot to pose as successful businesswomen—inventors of the Post-it Note!—to impress their former classmates at their reunion.

Virginia Woolf / *RuPaul's Drag Race* (22) In *Orlando*, a 1928 faux biography of Vita Sackville-West, Virginia Woolf explores the amorphous nature of gender in ways that resonate as strongly today as ever before. Andre Charles, a.k.a. RuPaul, is a modern-day exemplar of how clothing affects who we are and what we appear to be, and RuPaul's reality show *Drag Race* celebrates the blurring of the lines between masculine and feminine.

 Richard Yates / *Blue Velvet* (101) In Richard Yates's 1961 novel, *Revolutionary Road*, an unhappily married suburban couple dreams of leaving Connecticut behind and running off to Paris, where life just has to be better and more exciting. David Lynch's 1986 film stars future *Twin Peaks'* lead Kyle MacLachlan as an innocent college kid who returns to his childhood home to find that behind so many boring or cozy exteriors of the suburbs lies unspeakable—yet exciting!—depravity.

 Stefan Zweig / *Titanic* (132) James Cameron's 1997 blockbuster film may not have the happiest of conclusions (let's not pretend we don't know how *Titanic* ends!!), but at the apex of its romantic moments, it soars. Leonardo DiCaprio and Kate Winslet play Jack and Rose, young lovers from opposite ends of the economic spectrum and opposite ends of the literal boat who find each other briefly but intimately enough to feel like kings of the world. *The Post-Office Girl*, by Austrian writer Stefan Zweig, is the sad story of a destitute young woman who gets a peek at the good life when her wealthy American relatives invite her to travel with them for a brief holiday. Her misery grows deeper when she must return home after having experienced so briefly so much promise, now sensing that the life she glimpsed will always be just out of reach.

ACKNOWLEDGMENTS

Much love to everyone at Tumblr, but especially to book guru/beautiful genius/ life coach Rachel Fershleiser.

Huge thanks to Dan Greenberg and Tim Wojcik, and to all of the great people at Flatiron Books, including my wonderful editors, Colin Dickerman and James Melia, as well as Bob Miller, Marlena Bittner, Emily Walters, Elizabeth Van Itallie, and my beloved Liz Keenan.

Alex Naidus, thank you for being inspiring in every way.

For your encouragement and friendship, thank you to Jason Diamond, Amanda Bullock, Jami Attenberg, Elisa Albert, Emma Straub, Emily Gould, Christopher Schelling, Liz Scheier, Rachel Syme, Megan Lynch, John Sellers, Alexander Chee, Ryan Chapman, Summer Smith, Maud Newton, Yaniv Soha, Tyler Coates, Jen Doll, Bex Schwartz, Terra Chalberg, Heidi Metcalfe, Serena Jones, Jonathan Jao, Wylie O'Sullivan, Dorothy Robinson, Julia Cheiffetz, Drew Grant, Ami Greko, Miriam Parker, Kevin Nguyen, Megan Fitzpatrick, Kate McKean, Jenn Northington, Steph Opitz, and Lisa Lucas.

Thanks to Kera Bolonik, Austin Kleon, Sari Botton, Isaac Fitzgerald, Willa Paskin, Gabe Delahaye, Erica Cerulo, and Ruth Baron.

Group hug to Yancey Strickler and all of my friends at Kickstarter.

Thanks to Miwa Messer and Bill Tipper at B&N, and so much gratitude to Rachel Klayman, Liz Stein, Amy Scheibe, Martha Levin, Dominick Anfuso, and Lara Heimert.

Thanks to Rebecca Kirsch and Maureen Cesario, and to my family: Seth, Stacy, Sydney, Spencer, Jay, Marianne, and Sammi.

Josh Gondelman, you always make me feel so sane in the most glorious, colorful, and crazy way. I love you.

Mom, Dad, and Mookie: this is for you.

PERMISSIONS

Grateful acknowledgment is made for permission to reproduce from the following:

Gwyneth Paltrow: Photo by Pascal Le Segretain/Getty Images

The Great Muppet Caper: Universal Pictures/Photofest

There's Something About Mary: 20th Century Fox/Photofest/Glenn Watson

Gilmore Girls: Everett Collection

Parks and Recreation: Mitchell Haaseth/NBC/NBCU Photo Bank

The Good Wife: CBS/Photofest

The Goonies: Amblin Entertainment/Warner Bros./Photofest

Homeland: Showtime/Photofest

The Bachelor: ABC/Photofest

South Park: Bigger, Longer & Uncut: Paramount/Photofest

Lady Gaga: Kevin Winter/Getty Images

The Shining: Warner Bros. Pictures/Photofest

Before Sunrise: Castle Rock Entertainment/Photofest

Bob's Burgers: Fox/Photofest

Madonna: Everett Collection

Orange Is the New Black: Everett Collection

True Detective: HBO/Photofest

Boogie Nights: New Line Cinema/Photofest

Clint Eastwood at the Republican National Convention: Mark Wilson/Getty Images

Breaking Bad (Jesse Pinkman): AMC/Photofest

Tom Cruise: Courtesy of Landov Media

Lost in Translation: Focus Features/Photofest COPYRIGHT_NOTICE: © Focus Features

Dawson's Creek: The WB/Photofest

Harold & Kumar Go to White Castle: New Line Cinema/Photofest

Fargo: Gramercy Pictures/Photofest

The Wire: HBO/Photofest

Twin Peaks (Laura Palmer): ABC/Photofest

The Daily Show: Paul Hawthorne/Getty Images

The Golden Girls: Gary Null/NBC/NBCU Photo Bank via Getty Images

The Royal Tenenbaums: Touchstone Pictures/Photofest

Brokeback Mountain: © Focus Features Photographer: Kimberly French

Seinfeld (Jerry): NBC/Photofest

Bruce Springsteen: Photofest

Louie: Photofest

Lance Armstrong: Sony Pictures Classics/Photofest

Scandal: Richard Cartwright/ABC via Getty Images

The Big Lebowski: Gramercy Pictures/Photofest

Black Swan: Fox Searchlight Pictures/Photofest

Sex and the City: HBO/Photofest

The Office: Chris Haston/NBC/NBCU Photo Bank via Getty Images

Game of Thrones: HBO/Photofest

Six Feet Under: HBO/Photofest

Buffy the Vampire Slayer: The WB Television Network/Photofest

Beyoncé: Michael Buckner/Getty Images

Star Wars: © & TM Lucasfilm Ltd.

Pulp Fiction: Miramax/Photofest

Jersey Shore: Bobby Bank/WireImage

Donald Trump: NBC/Photofest

Trading Places: Paramount Pictures/Photofest

Hedwig and the Angry Inch: New Line Cinema/Photofest

White Chicks: Revolution/Columbia/Photofest

Heathers: New World Pictures/Photofest

Kill Bill: Volume 1: Miramax/Photofest

The Hunger Games: Lionsgate/Photofest

House of Cards: A-Pix Entertainment/Photofest

Tina Fey and Amy Poehler: NBC/Photofest

Anna Nicole Smith (1967–2007), circa 1995: Photo by The LIFE Picture Collection/
Getty Images

Say Anything: 20th Century Fox/Photofest

Miley Cyrus at the VMAs: Jeff Kravitz/FilmMagic for MTV

Working Girl: 20th Century Fox/Photofest

The Wolf of Wall Street: Paramount Pictures/Photofest

Kanye West: Photofest

Roseanne: ABC/Photofest

Freaks and Geeks: NBCU Photo Bank via Getty

Romy and Michele's High School Reunion: Touchstone Pictures/Photofest

Glee: Fox Broadcasting/Photofest

Arrested Development (Lucille Bluth): Fox/Photofest

The Simpsons (Smithers and Burns): 20th Century Fox/Photofest
Pretty Little Liars: ABC Family/Photofest
The Silence of the Lambs: Orion/Photofest
The Wonder Years: ABC/Photofest
Blue Velvet: De Laurentiis Ent. Gr./Photofest
Mad Men (Don Draper): AMC/Photofest
Keeping Up with the Kardashians: E! Entertainment Television/Photofest
Beavis and Butthead: MTV/Photofest
The Matrix: Warner Bros./Photofest
Eternal Sunshine of the Spotless Mind: Focus Features/Photofest
Arrested Development (Tobias): Fox/Photofest
Daria: Everett Collection
Waiting to Exhale: 20th Century Fox/Photofest
30 Rock: Ali Goldstein/NBC/NBCU Photo Bank via Getty Images
Mark Zuckerberg gives the keynote address at the South By Southwest Interactive
Festival on March 9, 2008 in Austin, Texas: Photo by Gary Miller/FilmMagic
Morrissey: Stephen Wright/Redferns via Getty
Wayne's World: NBC/Photofest
Thelma and Louise: MGM/Photofest
Veronica Mars: CBS/Photofest
Alias: ABC/Photofest
The Osbournes: Dave Hogan/Getty Images
Mrs. Doubtfire: 20th Century Fox/Photofest
Bill Clinton and Monica Lewinsky: © Dirck Halstead/Time Magazine/Gamma Liaison
The OC: Saeed Adyani/Warner Bros./Getty Images
Girls (Hannah and Jessa): HBO/Photofest
Prince: Warner Bros./Photofest
Gossip Girl: The CW/Photofest
Groundhog Day: Columbia Pictures/Photofest
The X-Files: 20th Century Fox/Photofest
Basic Instinct: TriStar/Photofest
Twin Peaks (The Log Lady): ABC/Photofest
Twilight: Summit Entertainment/Photofest
Titanic: Paramount Pictures/Photofest